SURVIVAL ENGLISH

English Through Conversations

Book 1

SECOND EDITION

Lee Mosteller

Bobbi Paul
San Diego Community Colleges

Illustrated by Jesse Gonzales

PRENTICE HALL REGENTS

Acquisitions editor: *Nancy Leonhardt*
Electronic production/interior design: *Louise B. Capuano*
Cover design: *Marianne Frasco*
Pre-press buyer/scheduler: *Ray Keating*
Manufacturing buyer: *Lori Bulwin*

© 1994 by PRENTICE HALL REGENTS
A Pearson Education Company
Pearson Education
10 Bank Street, White Plains, NY 10606

Printed in the United States of America

28

ISBN 0-13-016635-9

Contents

10 COMMUNITY 234

ESSENTIAL VOCABULARY 234

DIALOGUES

Preface

This workbook has been designed by teachers of beginning ESL students. It is aimed towards students who have some degree of literacy and does not address preliterate skills. To be successful with this book, students should have a small oral vocabulary and a knowledge of our alphabet.

The main objective of *Survival English* is to teach the most basic functional English patterns to these students. The teaching consists of many small steps that are simple, direct, and repetitive. Because of this, a few of the dialogues will not be conversationally functional. However, the book will provide a vocabulary and structure background in which new knowledge can be integrated.

Theoretically we agree that beginning students should have generous time to develop listening skills before being expected to produce language. However, the need exists to teach literacy as soon as possible along with oral skills, and as adults, these students want to read and write immediately.

Included in each unit is a variety of exercises to reinforce the oral patterns and to teach listening, speaking, reading, and writing. Reading and writing are introduced after the student has mastered oral patterns. This book is based on the theory that students learn to speak English by listening, speaking, reading, and writing, in that order.

OBJECTIVES

1. To teach the most basic functional language patterns in survival situations.

2. To teach language patterns and vocabulary in a systematic and controlled manner.

3. To develop reading and writing skills based on what the student can produce orally.

4. To provide survival information and coping skills necessary for adult living.

ACKNOWLEDGMENTS

Our special thanks to Gretchen Bitterlin, ESL Chairperson, San Diego Community Colleges, for her encouragement and suggestions.

SURVIVAL ENGLISH

1 PERSONAL ID

Essential Vocabulary
....

1. good morning
   how are you
   I'm fine
   thank you
   thanks
   afternoon
   evening

2. is
   she
   busy
   she's
   they
   they're
   happy
   tired
   hot
   cold
   sad
   angry

3. am
   he

4. isn't
   aren't
   no

5. not

6. what's
   her
   name
   Ann Lee
   his
   Bob Jones
   first
   last

7. your
   my
   spell that
   please
   middle
   maiden

8. address
   Main Street
   telephone number
   social security number

9. (review)

10. city
    state
    country
    zip code
    what

11. from
Mexico
Carbo

12. old
birth date
it's
year
month
January
February
March
April
May
June

July
August
September
October
November
December

13. married
widowed
husband
died

14. single
divorced

A.   Good morning.
         How are you?
B.   I'm fine, thank you.
         How are you?
A.   Fine, thanks.

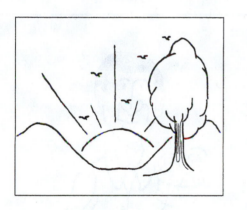

1.   Good morning.

2.   Good afternoon.

3.   Good evening.

1.   I   2.   we

3.   he   4.   you

5.   she   6.   they

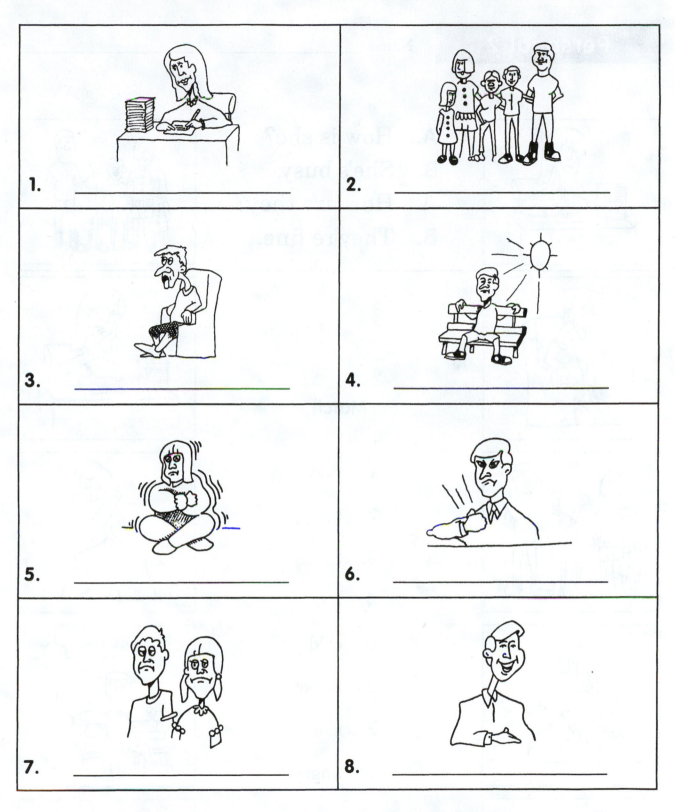

1. _____

2. _____

3. _____

4. _____

5. _____

6. _____

7. _____

8. _____

1. She's busy.

2. They're fine.

3. He's tired.

4. He's hot.

5. She's cold.

6. He's angry.

7. They're sad.

8. He's happy.

A. How is she?
B. She's busy.
A. How are they?
B. They're fine.

Match

1. fine

2. busy

3. tired

4. hot

5. cold

6. happy

7. sad

8. angry

How	are	you they	?		I'm They're	fine.
	is	he she			He's She's	

1. How is she?

_____ cold.

2. How is he?

_____ tired.

3. How are they?

_____ fine.

4. How is he?

_____ hot.

1. How is she?

She's _____.

2. How are they?

They're _____.

3. How is he?

He's _____.

4. How is he?

He's _____.

8

I'm They're	
He's She's	fine.

1. How is he?   _____ _____ .

2. How are they?   _____ _____ .

3. How are you?   _____ _____ .

4. How is she?   _____ _____ .

5. How are they?   _____ _____ .

6. How is he?   _____ _____ .

7. How are you?   _____ _____ .

8. How is she?   _____ _____ .

A. Are you busy?
B. Yes, I am.
A. Is he tired?
B. Yes, he is.

1. Are you busy?

Yes, _____ am.

2. Is he tired?

Yes, _____ is.

3. Are they happy?

Yes, _____ are.

Yes,	I	am.
	he she	is.
	they	are.

1. Is she busy?

Yes, _____ _____ .

2. Is he tired?

Yes, _____ _____ .

3. Are they sad?

Yes, _____ _____ .

4. Are you busy?

Yes, _____ _____ .

A. Is he sad?

B. No, he isn't.

A. Are they happy?

B. No, they aren't.

1. Are they happy?

No, _____ aren't.

2. Is he sad?

No, _____ isn't.

3. Is she tired?

No, _____ isn't.

No,	he she	isn't.
	they	aren't.

1. Is he happy?

No, _____ _____ .

2. Are they sad?

No, _____ _____ .

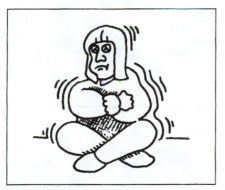

3. Is she hot?

No, _____ _____ .

4. Is he angry?

No, _____ _____ .

1. Is he cold?

   No, _____ _____ .

2. Are they happy?

   Yes, _____ _____ .

3. Is he hot?

   No, _____ _____ .

4. Is she cold?

   Yes, _____ _____ .

14

A. Are you busy?
B. No, I'm not.

---

1. Are you busy? No, I'm not.

2. Are you angry? No, I'm _____ .

3. Are you cold? No, I'm _____ .

4. Are you hot? No, _____ _____ .

5. Are you sad? _____ , _____ _____ .

6. Are you fine? Yes, I am.

7. Are you busy? Yes, I _____ .

8. Are you happy? Yes, I _____ .

9. Are you tired? Yes, _____ _____ .

10. Are you cold? _____ , _____ _____ .

A. What's her name?

B. Her first name is Ann.

Her last name is Lee.

A. What's his name?

B. His first name is Bob.

His last name is Jones.

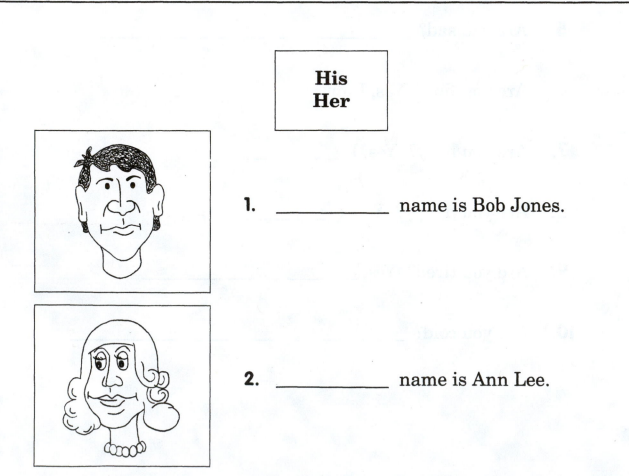

| **His** |
| **Her** |

1. _____ name is Bob Jones.

2. _____ name is Ann Lee.

Bob Jones

1. His _____ name is Bob.

   His _____ name is Jones.

Ann Lee

2. Her _____ name is Ann.

   Her _____ name is Lee.

you

3. My first name is _____ .

   My last name is _____ .

A. What's your name?

B. My name is _____ .

A. What's your first name?

B. My first name is _____ .

A. Spell that.

B. _____

A. What's your last name?

B. My last name is _____ .

A. Please spell that.

B. _____

_____

First name _____ Middle name _____

Last name _____ Maiden name _____

Last name _____

First name _____

Middle name _____

Maiden name _____

Name _____
　　　　Last　　　　　　　　First　　　　　　　Middle

A. What's his address?

B. 7613 Main Street.

A. What's his telephone number?

B. 560–6660.

A. What's his Social Security number?

B. 560–58–8025.

Match

1. address

2. telephone number

3. Social Security number

4. address

5. telephone number

6. address

7. Social Security number

8. telephone number

9. address

10. Social Security number

11. telephone number

12. address

First name _____

1. _____   2. _____   3. _____ – __ – _____

A. What's your address?

B. _____

A. What's your telephone number?

B. _____

A. What's your Social Security number?

B. _____

_____

Name _____   NAME _____

Add. _____   ADDRESS _____

Tel. _____   TELEPHONE _____

Soc. Sec. No. _____ – __ – _____   SOCIAL SECURITY _____ – __ – _____

name _____   Name _____

address _____   Address _____

telephone _____   Telephone _____

social security _____ – __ – _____   Social Security _____ – __ – _____

First name _____

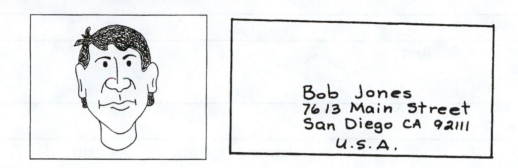

Bob Jones
7613 Main Street
San Diego CA 92111
U.S.A.

A. What's your address?

B. _____

A. What city?

B. _____

A. What state?

B. _____

A. What country?

B. _____

A. What's your zip code?

B. _____

_____

address _____

city _____

state _____

zip code _____

```
Name        _____
                     first                          last

Address     _____

            _____
                 city              state              zip code

Telephone number    _____

Social Security number   _____  -  _____  -  _____
```

1. My first name is _____ .

2. My last name is _____ .

3. My address is _____ .

4. My telephone number is _____ .

5. My zip code is _____ .

6. My Social Security number is _____ - _____ - _____ .

7. My city is _____ .

8. My state is _____ .

9. My country is _____ .

Match

first name	560–58–8025
telephone number	San Diego
zip code	Jones
Social Security number	7613 Main Street
last name	92111
state	California
country	560–6660
city	U.S.A.
address	Bob

First name _____ Last name _____

Address _____

Country _____ City _____ State _____

Telephone number _____ Zip code _____

Social Security number _____ – ____ – _____

_____

last name   first name

_____

address   city   state

_____

country   zip code

_____

telephone number

A. What country is he from?

B. He's from Mexico.

A. What city is he from?

B. He's from Carbo.

A. What country are you from?

B. I'm from _____ .

A. What city are you from?

B. I'm from _____ .

I'm from _____ , _____ .

Name _____

Address _____
        street   city

_____
        state   zip code

Telephone _____

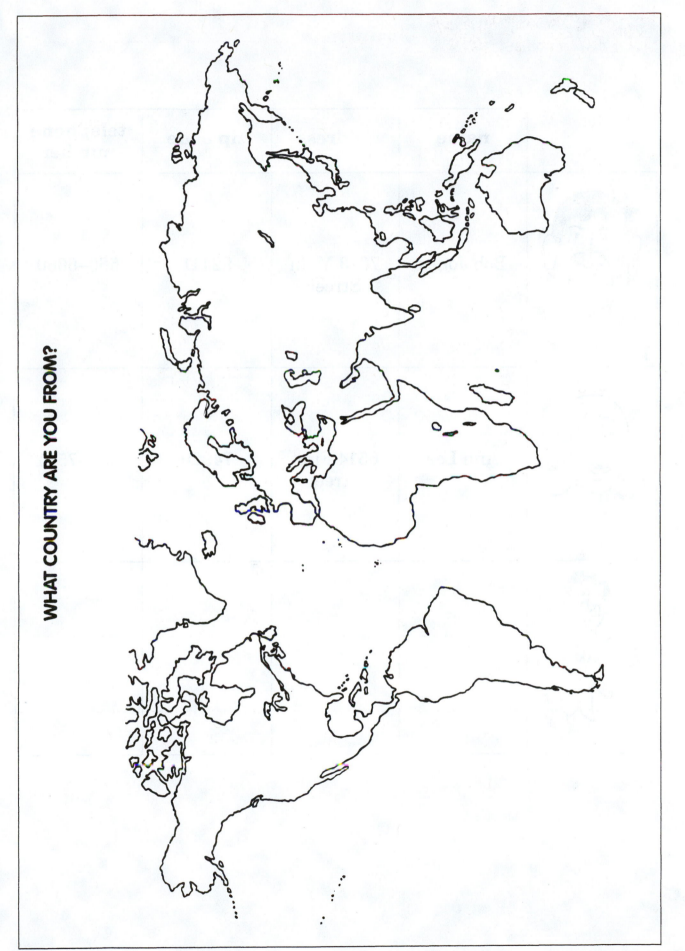

	name	address	zip code	telephone number
1.	Bob Jones	7613 Main Street	92111	560–6660
2.	Ann Lee	6514 First Street	74920	896–7531
3.				

A. How old is Bob?

B. He's 45.

A. What's his birth date?

B. It's May 17, 1948.

A. How old are you?

B. I'm _____ .

A. What's your birthdate?

B. It's _____ ____ , 19____ .

name	age	birth date		
		month	day	year
Bob Jones	45	May	17	1948

January
February
March
April
May
June
July
August
September
October
November
December

A. Is he married?

B. Yes, he is.

A. Is she married?

B. No, she isn't.

She's widowed.

Her husband died.

Yes,	he she	is.
	they	are.

No,	he she	isn't.
	they	aren't.

1. Is he married?

Yes, _____ _____ .

2. Is he widowed?

No, _____ _____ .

3. Are they married?

Yes, _____ _____ .

4. Is she widowed?

Yes, _____ _____ .

5. Is she married?

No, _____ _____ .

A. Is she married?

B. No, she isn't.
    She's single.

A. Is he married?

B. No, he isn't.
    He's divorced.

A. Are you married?

B. _____

1. Is she married?

No, _____ _____ .

2. Is she single?

Yes, _____ _____ .

3. Is he divorced?

No, _____ _____ .

4. Is he married?

Yes, _____ _____ .

5. Are they married?

No, _____ _____ .

6. Are they divorced?

Yes, _____ _____ .

Sue and Joe are married.
They're happy.
They're from Mexico.

---

1. Is Sue married?

   _____.

2. Is Joe married?

   _____.

3. Is Joe happy?

   _____.

4. Is Joe single?

   _____.

5. Is Sue single?

   _____.

6. What country are they from?

   _____.

7. Are they from Mexico?

   _____.

8. Are you married?

   _____.

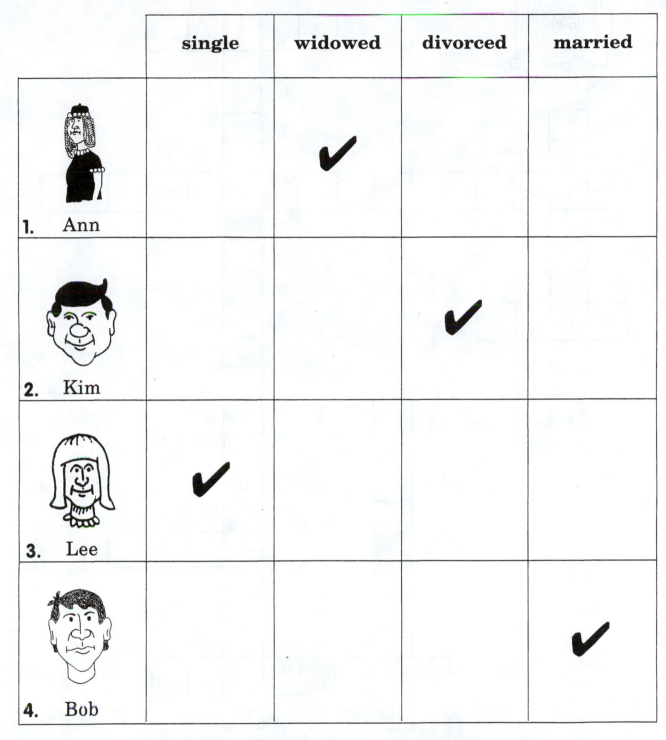

	single	widowed	divorced	married
1. Ann		✔		
2. Kim			✔	
3. Lee	✔			
4. Bob				✔

1. Is Bob married?

2. Is Bob divorced?

3. Is Lee single?

4. Is Lee married?

5. Is Ann divorced?

6. Is Ann widowed?

7. Is Kim married?

8. Is Kim single?

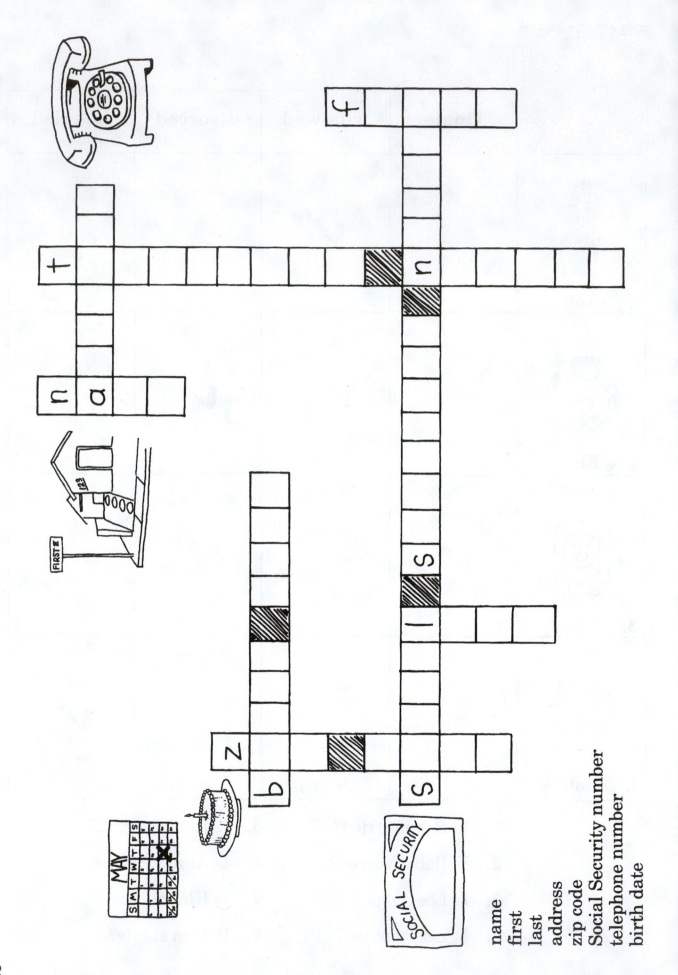

name
first
last
address
zip code
Social Security number
telephone number
birth date

 **GENERAL**

Essential Vocabulary

1. where's
    the
    on
    in
    next to
    under
    over
    between
    pencil sharpener
    pen
    light
    chair
    pencil
    clock
    door
    blackboard / chalkboard
    paper
    book
    table
    window

2. stand up
    walk
    close
    open
    go out
    come in
    sit down
    read
    write

3. today
    Sunday
    Monday
    Tuesday
    Wednesday
    Thursday
    Friday
    Saturday

4. yesterday
    tomorrow
    was

5. date

6. weather
    how's
    sunny
    rainy
    cloudy
    hot
    cold

7. excuse me
    time
    class
    at

8. need
penny
nickel
dime
quarter
dollar

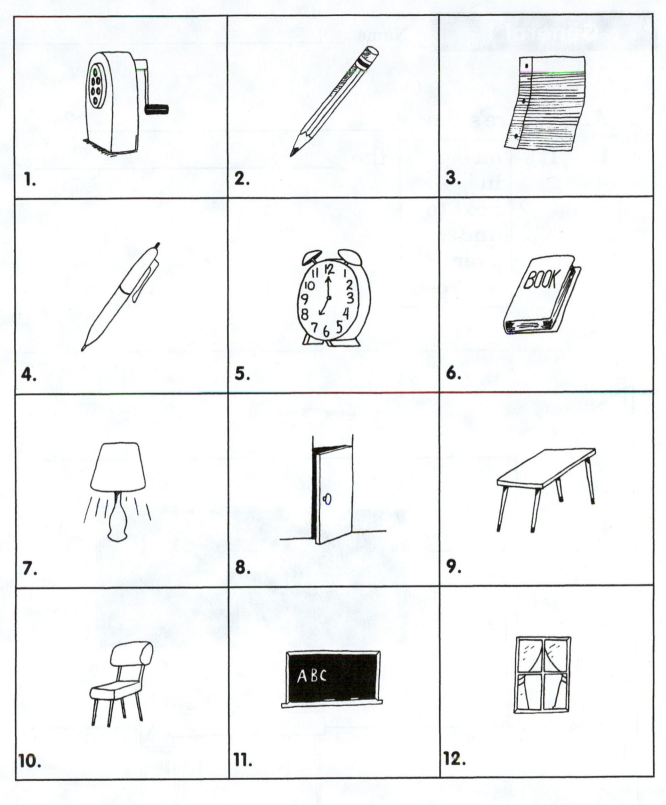

1.

2.

3.

4.

5.

6.

7.

8.

9.

10.

11.

12.

pencil sharpener	pencil	paper
pen	clock	book
light	door	table
chair	chalkboard / blackboard	window

General 1

Name ______________________

A. Where's the ______________________?

B. It's

on
in
next to
under
over
between

the ______________________.

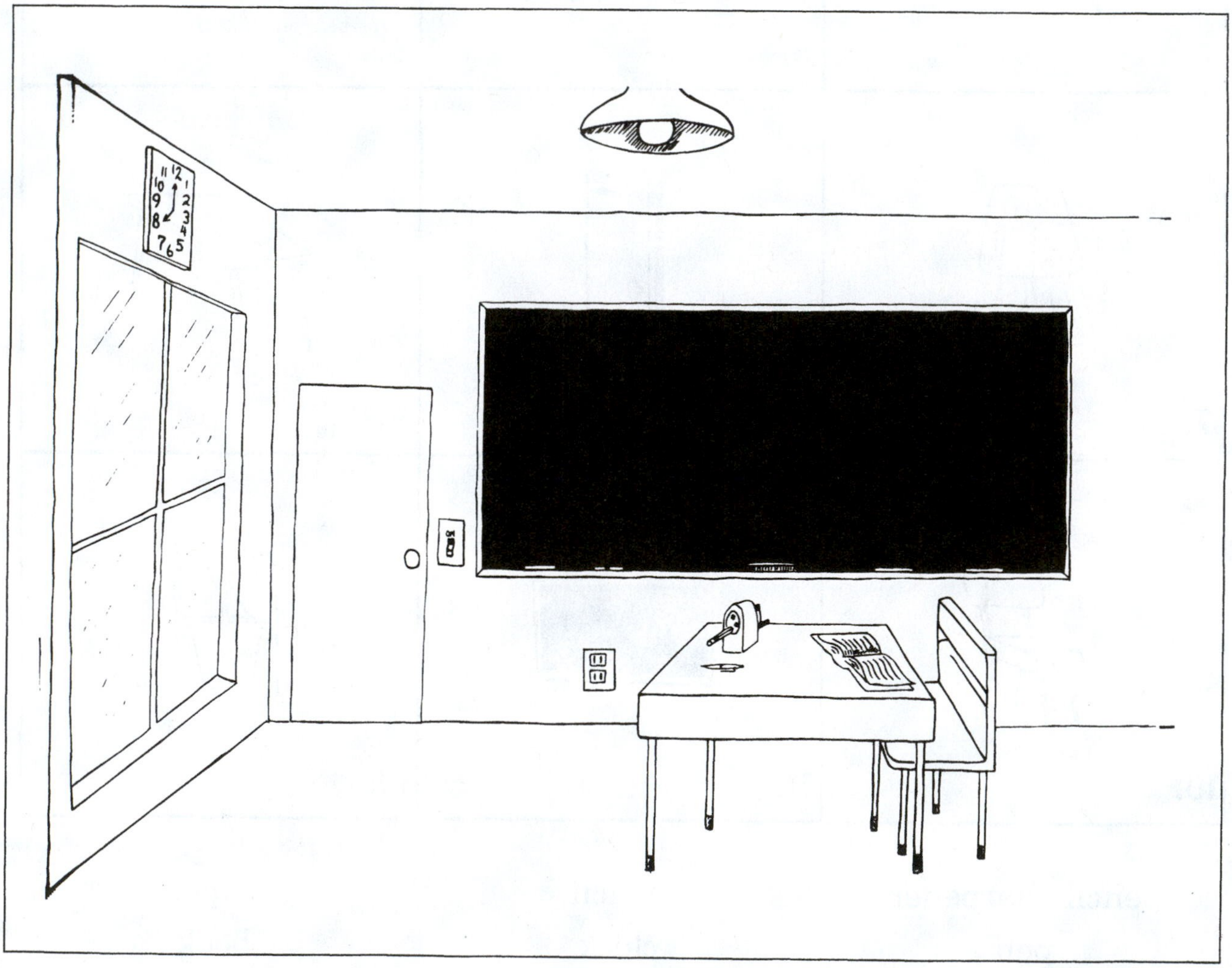

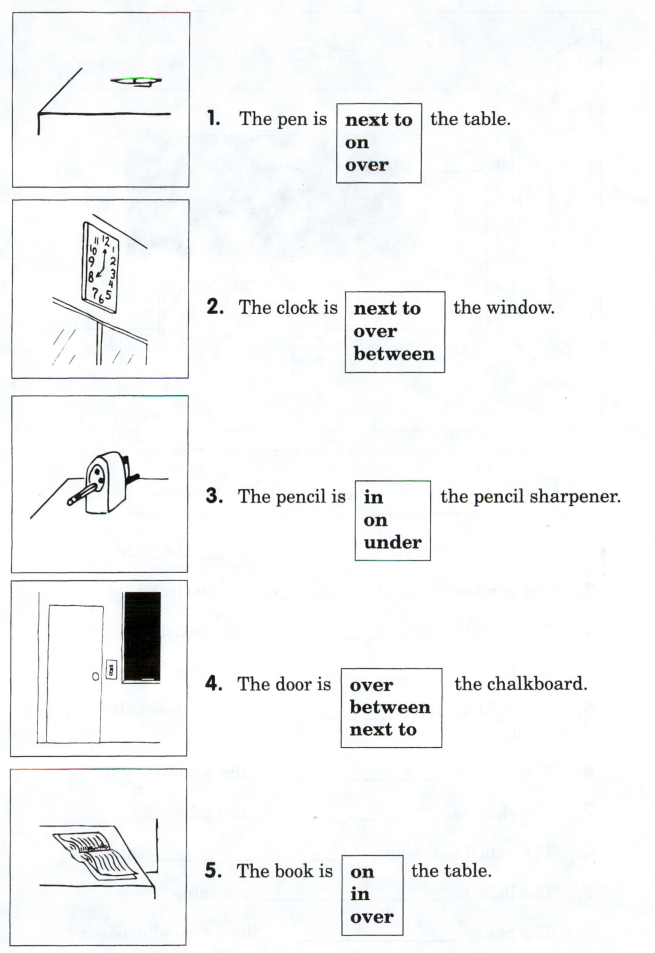

1. The pen is | **next to**
 on
 over | the table.

2. The clock is | **next to**
 over
 between | the window.

3. The pencil is | **in**
 on
 under | the pencil sharpener.

4. The door is | **over**
 between
 next to | the chalkboard.

5. The book is | **on**
 in
 over | the table.

on	next to	over
in	under	between

1. The light switch is _____ the door.

2. The window is _____ the clock.

3. The pencil is _____ the pencil sharpener.

4. The book is _____ the table.

5. The light switch is _____ the chalkboard and the door.

6. The clock is _____ the window.

7. The chair is _____ the table.

8. The pencil sharpener is _____ the table.

9. The light is _____ the table.

10. The pen is _____ the pencil sharpener.

1.

2.

3.

4.

5.

6.

go
stand
give

open
close
write

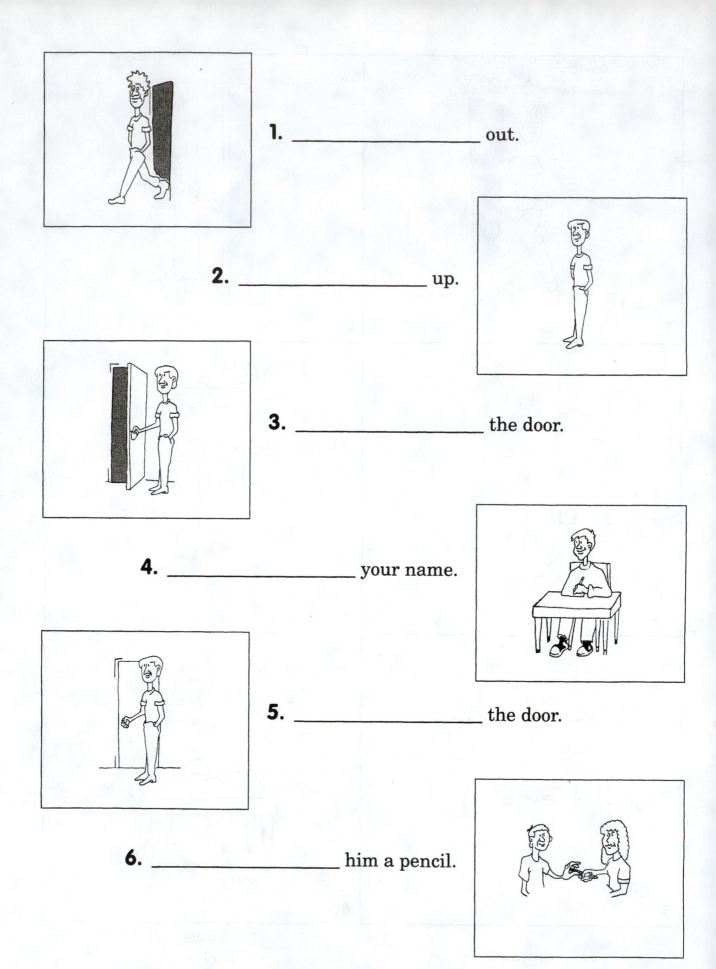

1. _____ out.

2. _____ up.

3. _____ the door.

4. _____ your name.

5. _____ the door.

6. _____ him a pencil.

1. Please stand up.
2. Please go to the door.
3. Please open the door.
4. Please go out.
5. Please come in.
6. Please close the door.
7. Please go to the window.
8. Please open the window.
9. Please close the window.
10. Please walk to your chair.
11. Please sit down.
12. Please open your book.
13. Please read your book.
14. Please close your book.
15. Please write your name.
    Thank you.

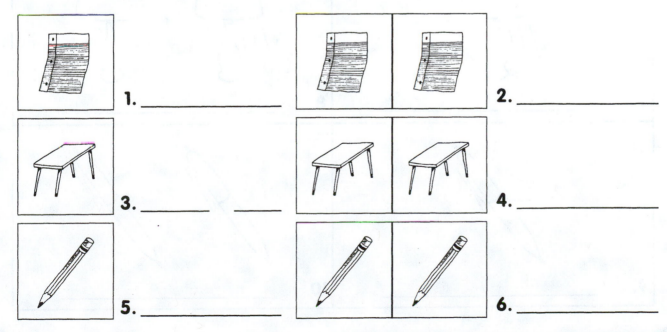

1. _____

2. _____

3. _____

4. _____

5. _____

6. _____

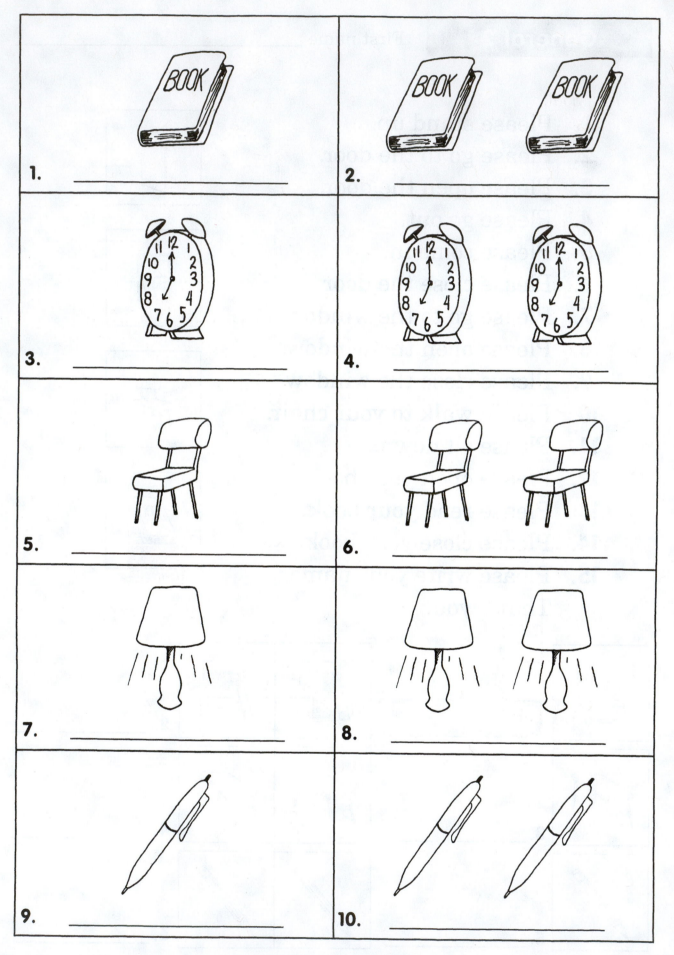

1. _____

2. _____

3. _____

4. _____

5. _____

6. _____

7. _____

8. _____

9. _____

10. _____

book
pencil sharpener
blackboard
paper
clock
table
door
light
pen
chair

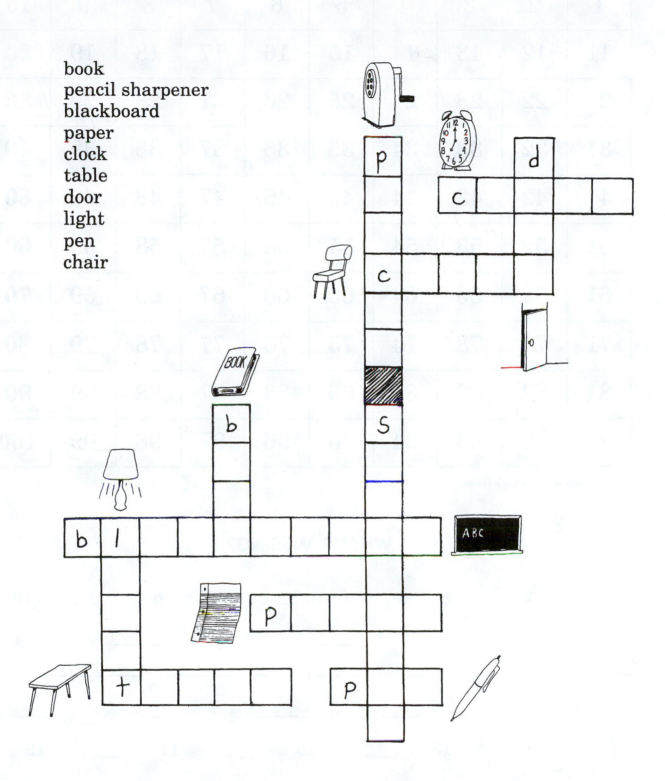

1	2	3	4	**5**	6	7	8	9	**10**
11	12	13	14	**15**	16	17	18	19	**20**
21	22	23	24	**25**	26	27	28	29	**30**
31	32	33	34	**35**	36	37	38	39	**40**
41	42	43	44	**45**	46	47	48	49	**50**
51	52	53	54	**55**	56	57	58	59	**60**
61	62	63	64	**65**	66	67	68	69	**70**
71	72	73	74	**75**	76	77	78	79	**80**
81	82	83	84	**85**	86	87	88	89	**90**
91	92	93	94	**95**	96	97	98	99	**100**

See the Teacher's Guide.

WHAT'S MISSING?

1   2   ___   4   5   ___   7   8   ___   10

11   ___   13   14   ___   16   17   ___   19

---

1   ___   3   ___   5   ___   7   ___   9   ___

11   ___   13   ___   15   ___   17   ___   19

___   21   ___   23   ___   25   ___   27   ___

29   ___   31   ___   33   ___   35   ___   37

10,   20,   ___   40,   50,   ___   70,   80,   ___   100

0	zero
1	one
2	two
3	three
4	four
5	five
6	six
7	seven
8	eight
9	nine
10	ten
11	eleven
12	twelve
13	thirteen
14	fourteen
15	fifteen
16	sixteen
17	seventeen
18	eighteen
19	nineteen
20	twenty
30	thirty
40	forty
50	fifty
60	sixty
70	seventy
80	eighty
90	ninety
100	one hundred

Last name _____

A. What's today?

B. It's _____ .

_____

1. Sunday _____ Sun. _____

2. Monday _____ Mon. _____

3. Tuesday _____ Tues. _____

4. Wednesday _____ Wed. _____

5. Thursday _____ Thur. _____

6. Friday _____ Fri. _____

7. Saturday _____ Sat. _____

A. What's today?

B. It's _____ .

A. What was yesterday?

B. It was _____ .

A. What's tomorrow?

B. It's _____ .

_____

1. Today is Monday.

Tomorrow is _____ .

2. Today is Wednesday.

Tomorrow is _____ .

3. Today is Friday.

Tomorrow is _____ .

4. Today is Friday.

Yesterday was _____ .

5. Today is Sunday.

Yesterday was _____ .

Address _____

A. What's the date?

B. It's _____ , _____ _____ .

---

1. January _____ Jan. _____

2. February _____ Feb. _____

3. March _____ Mar. _____

4. April _____ Apr. _____

5. May _____ May _____

6. June _____ Jun. _____

7. July _____ Jul. _____

8. August _____ Aug. _____

9. September _____ Sept. _____

10. October _____ Oct. _____

11. November _____ Nov. _____

12. December _____ Dec. _____

before	after

1. June is _____ May.

2. September is _____ August.

3. December is _____ November.

4. February is _____ January.

5. July is _____ August.

6. March is _____ May.

7. August is _____ July.

8. October is _____ November.

9. January is _____ February.

10. November is _____ December.

11. April is _____ March.

12. May is _____ June.

SEPTEMBER

Sun.	Mon.	Tues.	Wed.	Thurs.	Fri.	Sat.
		1	2	3	4	5
6	7	8	9	10	11	12
13	14	15	16	17	18	19
20	21	22	23	24	25	26
27	28	29	30			

See the Teacher's Guide.

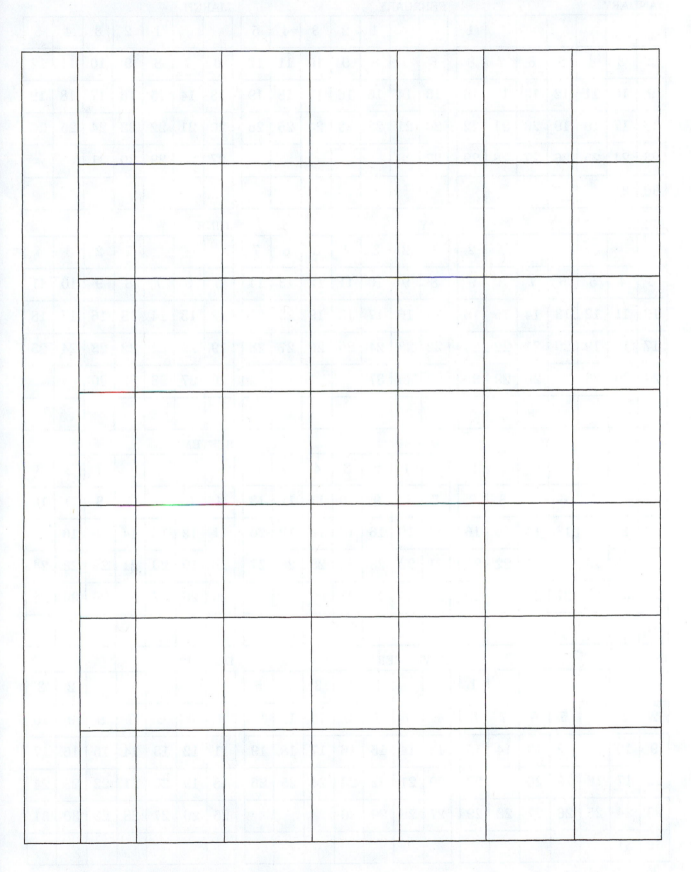

See the Teacher's Guide.

1994

JANUARY

						1
2	3	4	5	6	7	8
9	10	11	12	13	14	15
16	17	18	19	20	21	22
23	24	25	26	27	28	29
30	31					

FEBRUARY

	1	2	3	4	5
6	7	8	9	10	11	12
13	14	15	16	17	18	19
20	21	22	23	24	25	26
27	28					

MARCH

		1	2	3	4	5
6	7	8	9	10	11	12
13	14	15	16	17	18	19
20	21	22	23	24	25	26
27	28	29	30	31		

APRIL

					1	2
3	4	5	6	7	8	9
10	11	12	13	14	15	16
17	18	19	20	21	22	23
24	25	26	27	28	29	30

MAY

1	2	3	4	5	6	7
8	9	10	11	12	13	14
15	16	17	18	19	20	21
22	23	24	25	26	27	28
29	30	31				

JUNE

			1	2	3	4
5	6	7	8	9	10	11
12	13	14	15	16	17	18
19	20	21	22	23	24	25
26	27	28	29	30		

JULY

					1	2
3	4	5	6	7	8	9
10	11	12	13	14	15	16
17	18	19	20	21	22	23
24	25	26	27	28	29	30
31						

AUGUST

	1	2	3	4	5	6
7	8	9	10	11	12	13
14	15	16	17	18	19	20
21	22	23	24	25	26	27
28	29	30	31			

SEPTEMBER

				1	2	3
4	5	6	7	8	9	10
11	12	13	14	15	16	17
18	19	20	21	22	23	24
25	26	27	28	29	30	

OCTOBER

						1
2	3	4	5	6	7	8
9	10	11	12	13	14	15
16	17	18	19	20	21	22
23	24	25	26	27	28	29
30	31					

NOVEMBER

	1	2	3	4	5
6	7	8	9	10	11	12
13	14	15	16	17	18	19
20	21	22	23	24	25	26
27	28	29	30			

DECEMBER

				1	2	3
4	5	6	7	8	9	10
11	12	13	14	15	16	17
18	19	20	21	22	23	24
25	26	27	28	29	30	31

See the Teacher's Guide.

First name _____

A. How's the weather?

B. It's rainy.

sunny

 cloudy

rainy

hot / cold

1. How's the weather?

   It's _____ .

2. How's the weather?

   It's _____ .

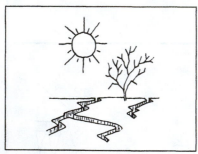

3. How's the weather?

   It's _____ .

4. How's the weather?

   It's _____ .

5. How's the weather?

   It's _____ .

6. How's the weather?

   It's _____ .

Last name _____

A. Excuse me. What time is it?

B. It's 8:00.

A. What time is the class?

B. It's at 8:30.

See the Teacher's Guide.

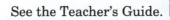

WHAT TIME IS IT?

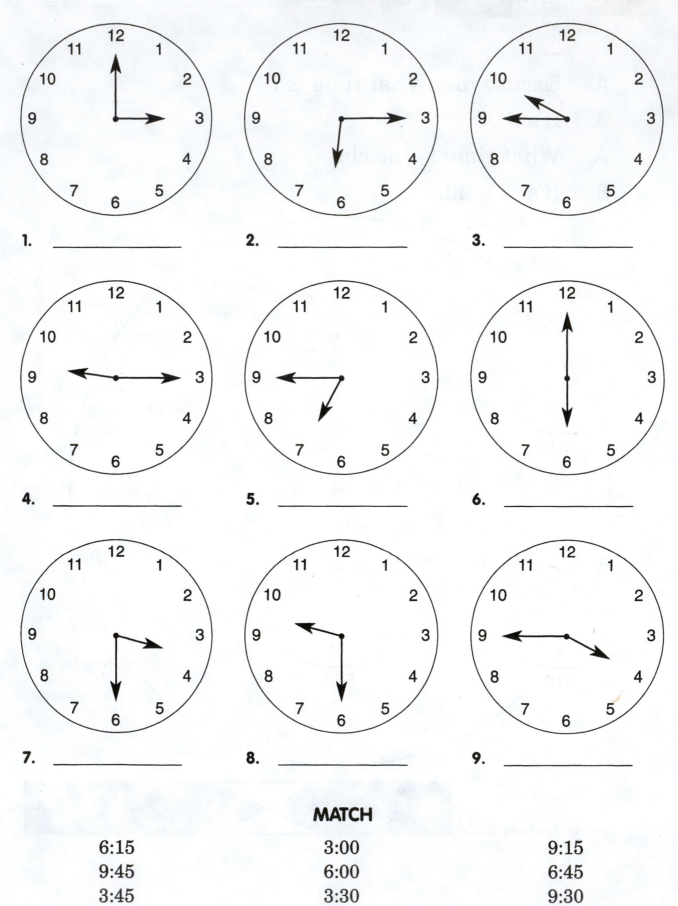

1. _____

2. _____

3. _____

4. _____

5. _____

6. _____

7. _____

8. _____

9. _____

MATCH

6:15	3:00	9:15
9:45	6:00	6:45
3:45	3:30	9:30

WHAT TIME IS IT?

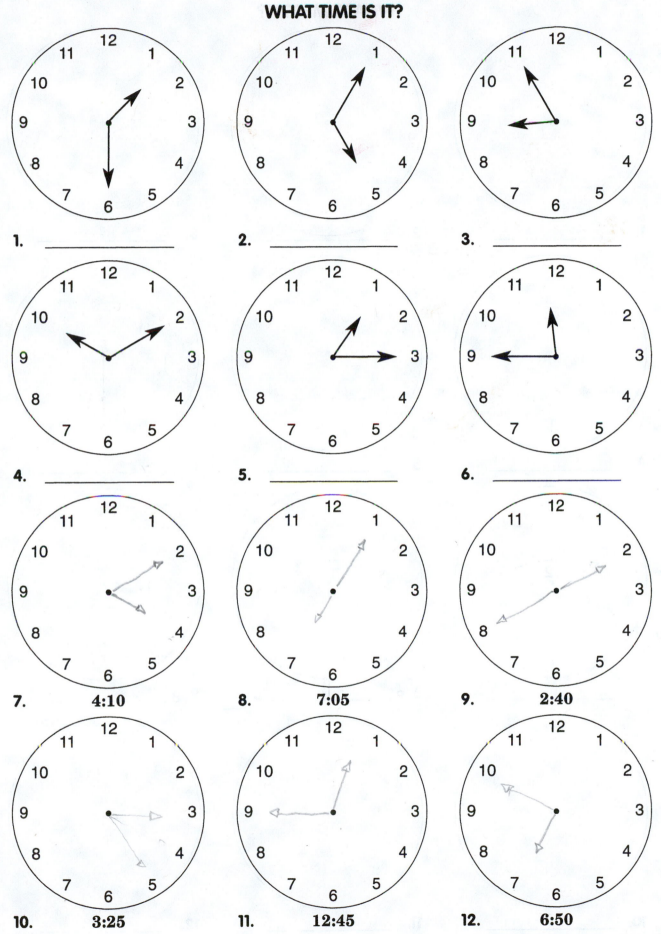

1. _____

2. _____

3. _____

4. _____

5. _____

6. _____

7.   **4:10**

8.   **7:05**

9.   **2:40**

10.   **3:25**

11.   **12:45**

12.   **6:50**

WHAT TIME IS IT?

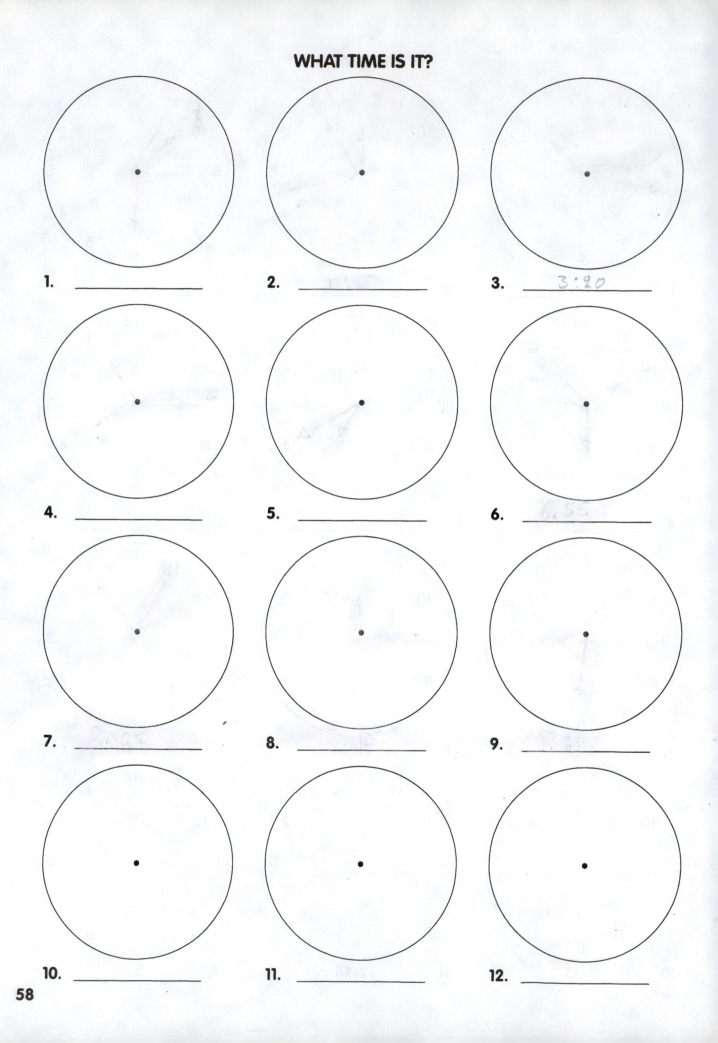

1. _____

2. _____

3. ___3:20___

4. _____

5. _____

6. ___6.55___

7. _____

8. _____

9. _____

10. _____

11. _____

12. _____

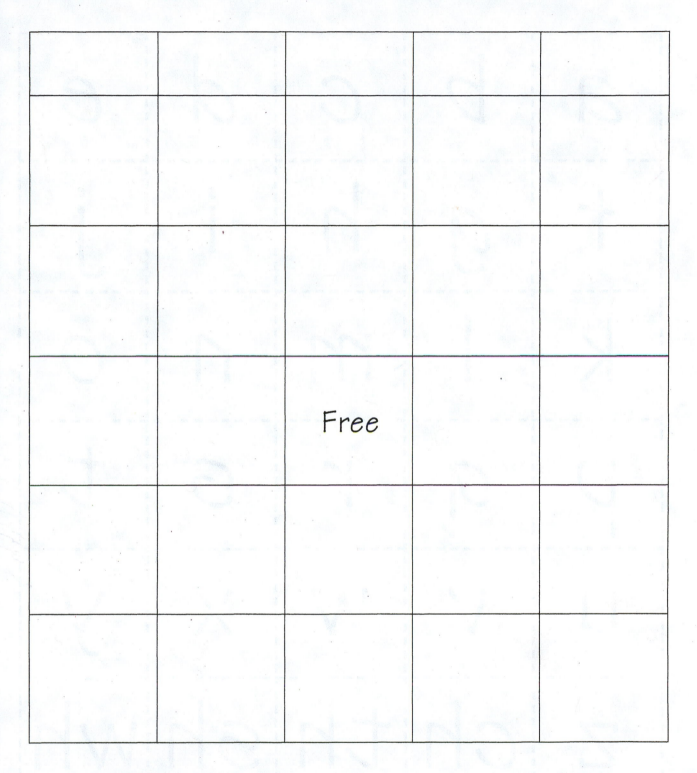

Free

See the Teacher's Guide.

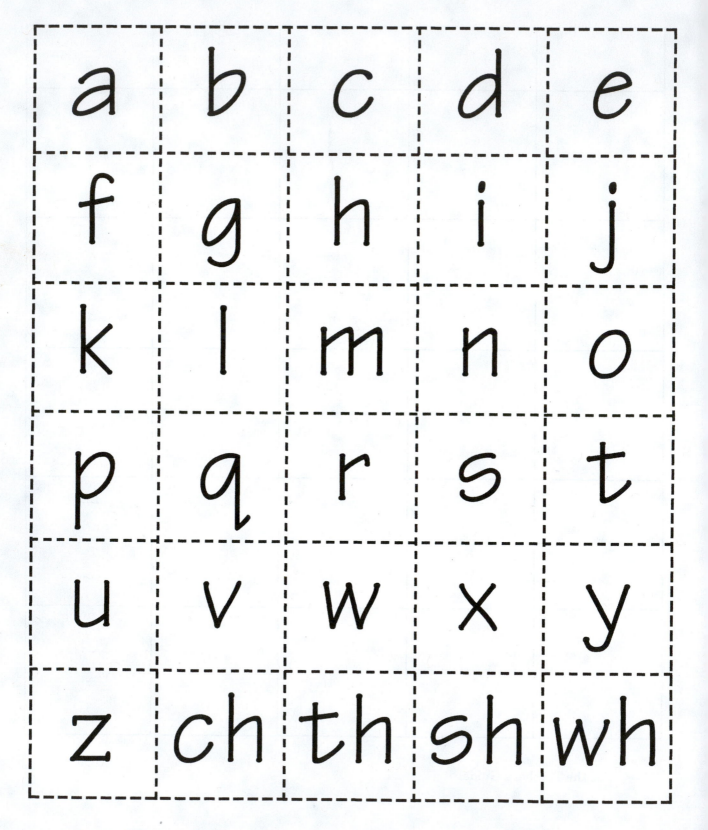

a	b	c	d	e
f	g	h	i	j
k	l	m	n	o
p	q	r	s	t
u	v	w	x	y
z	ch	th	sh	wh

See the Teacher's Guide.

WHAT'S MISSING?

1. a b ___ d e f ___ h i j k ___ m n ___ p q ___
    s ___ u ___ w x ___ z

2. A ___ C D ___ F G ___ I ___ K L M ___ O
    P ___ R ___ T U ___ W ___ Y ___

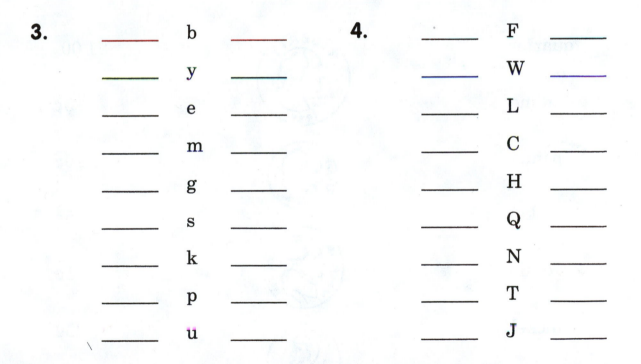

3. ___ b   ___
    ___ y   ___
    ___ e   ___
    ___ m   ___
    ___ g   ___
    ___ s   ___
    ___ k   ___
    ___ p   ___
    ___ u   ___

4. ___ F   ___
    ___ W   ___
    ___ L   ___
    ___ C   ___
    ___ H   ___
    ___ Q   ___
    ___ N   ___
    ___ T   ___
    ___ J   ___

A.   I need a _____ .

1. quarter
25¢

2. dime
10¢

3. nickel
5¢

4. penny
1¢

5. dollar
$1.00

MATCH

quarter		$1.00
dime		5¢
penny		10¢
nickel		25¢
dime		1¢
nickel		25¢
quarter		5¢
penny		10¢
dollar		1¢

penny	nickel	dime	quarter
1¢	5¢	10¢	25¢

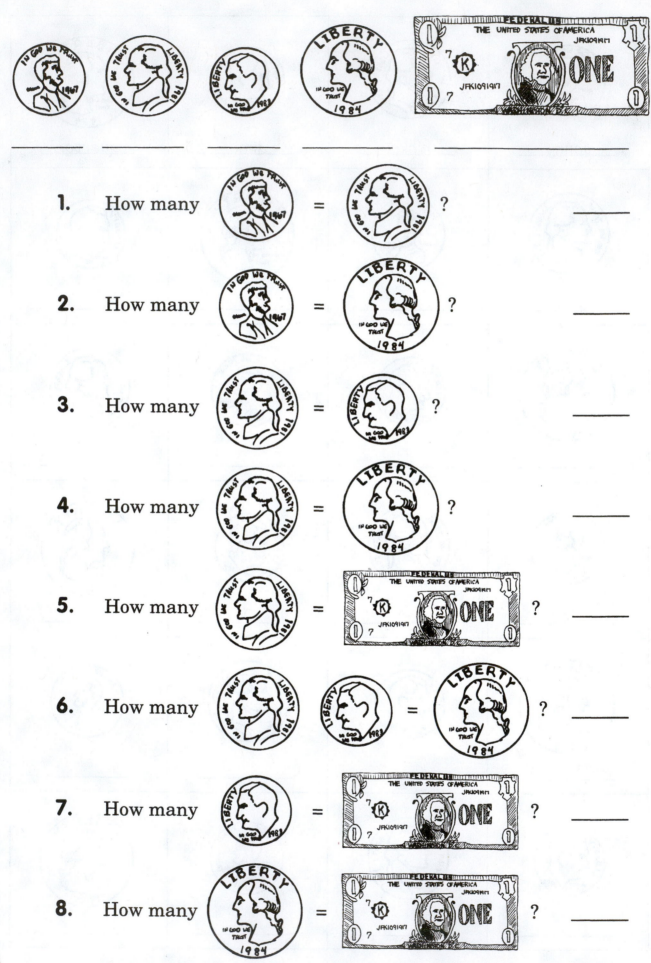

1. How many [penny] = [nickel] ? _____

2. How many [penny] = [quarter] ? _____

3. How many [nickel] = [dime] ? _____

4. How many [nickel] = [quarter] ? _____

5. How many [nickel] = [one dollar] ? _____

6. How many [nickel] [dime] = [quarter] ? _____

7. How many [dime] = [one dollar] ? _____

8. How many [quarter] = [one dollar] ? _____

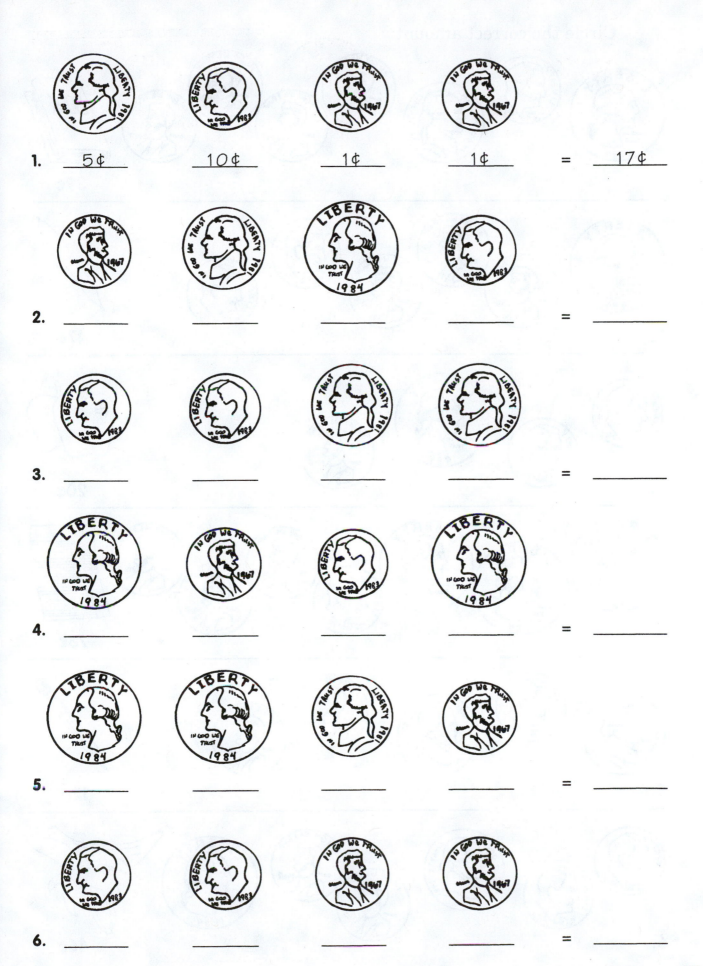

1. 5¢   10¢   1¢   1¢   =   17¢

2. _____   _____   _____   =   _____

3. _____   _____   _____   =   _____

4. _____   _____   _____   =   _____

5. _____   _____   _____   =   _____

6. _____   _____   _____   =   _____

Circle the correct amount:

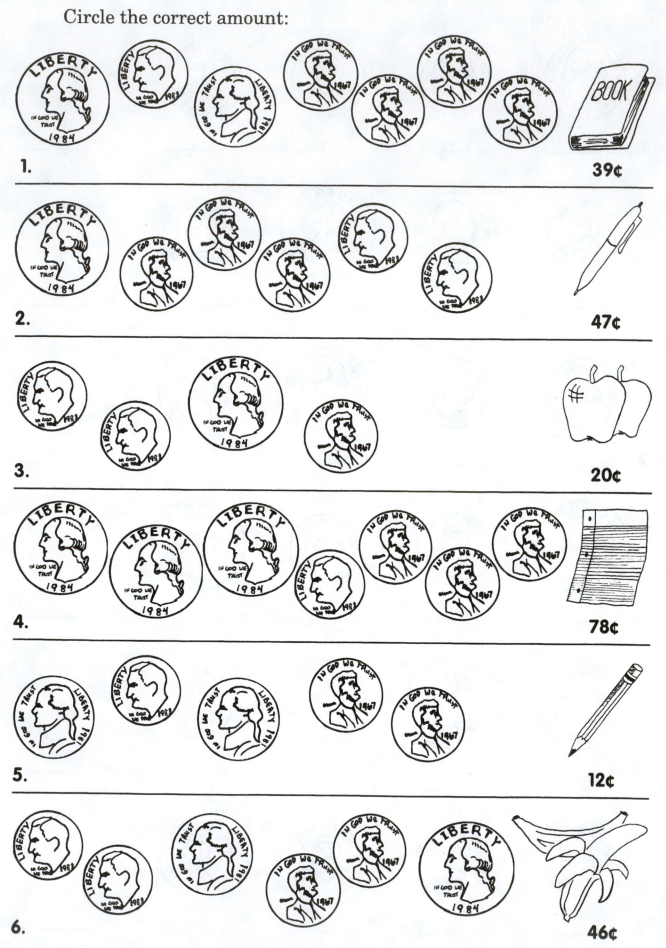

1.   39¢

2.   47¢

3.   20¢

4.   78¢

5.   12¢

6.   46¢

Essential Vocabulary

1. who's
   wife
   sister
   mother
   father
   brother
   friend
   too

2. store

3. husband
   home
   doing
   taking care of
   children
   cooking
   cleaning
   studying
   now

4. doesn't
   does
   have

   how many
   has
   sons
   daughters

5. do
   don't

6. school
   child
   one

7. kindergarten
   elementary
   grade
   teacher
   high school
   junior high
   Mrs.

8. student
   Miss
   Mr.
   Ms.

9. excited
why
because
coming
parents
grandparents
grandsons
granddaughters
grandchildren

A.   Who's she?

B.   She's my wife.

A.   Is she your sister?

B.   No, she isn't. She's my mother.

A.   Is he your father?

B.   No, he isn't. He's my brother.

A.   Is he your brother too?

B.   No, he isn't. He's my friend.

mother

brother

friend

wife

husband

wife	husband
sister	brother
mother	father
grandmother	grandfather
aunt	uncle
cousin	cousin
friend	friend

1. My name is _____ .

2. My mother's name is _____ .

3. My father's name is _____ .

4. My grandfather's name is _____ .

5. My grandmother's name is _____ .

6. My sister's name is _____ .

7. My brother's name is _____ .

8. My uncle's name is _____ .

9. My aunt's name is _____ .

10. My friend's name is _____ .

11. My teacher's name is _____ .

A.   Where's your wife?

B.   She's at the store.

_____

1.    Where's your husband?

_____

2.    Where are your children?

_____

3.    Where's your brother?

_____

A. Where's your husband?

B. He's at home.

A. What's he doing?

B. He's taking care of the children now.

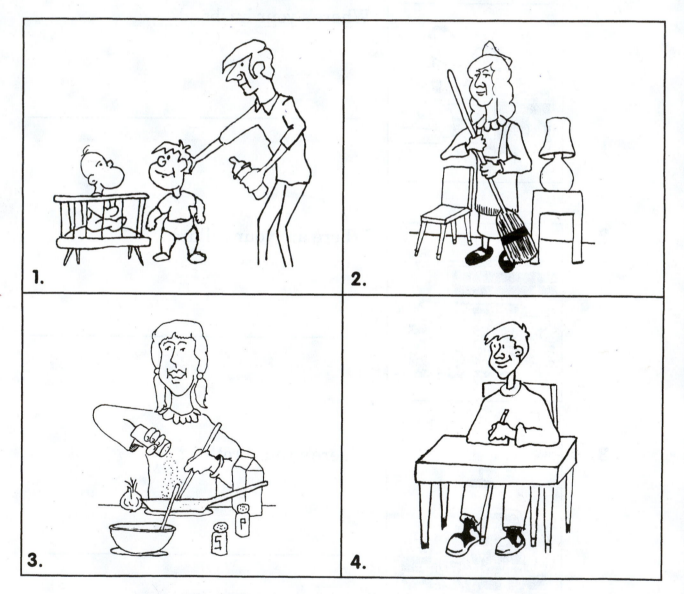

taking care of
cooking

cleaning
studying

Yes,	he she	is.		He's She's

1. Is he at home?

_____ , _____ _____ .

What's he doing?

_____ _____ _____

_____ _____ .

2. Is she at home?

_____ , _____ _____ .

What's she doing?

_____ _____ .

3. Is she at home?

_____ , _____ _____ .

What's she doing?

_____ _____ _____ _____

4. Is he at home?

_____ , _____ _____ .

What's he doing?

_____ _____

No,	he she	isn't.

1. Is he studying?

No, _____ _____ .

He's _____ _____ _____

_____ _____ .

2. Is she cleaning the house?

No, _____ _____ .

She's _____ .

3. Is he taking care of the children?

No, _____ _____ .

He's _____ .

4. Is she cooking?

No, _____ _____ .

She's _____ .

A. Does he have children?

B. No, he doesn't.

A. Does she have children?

B. Yes, she does.

A. How many children does she have?

B. She has 5 children.

She has 3 sons and 2 daughters.

Yes,	he she	does.

He She	has

1. Does she have children?

_____ , _____ _____ .

2. How many children does she have?

_____ _____ _____ _____ .

3. Does he have children?

_____ , _____ _____ .

4. How many children does he have?

_____ _____ _____ _____ .

Zip code _____

A. Do you have children?

B. No, I don't. I'm single.

Do you have children?

A. Yes, I do.

B. How many children do you have?

A. I have _____ children.

---

1. Do you have children?

_____ , I _____ .

2. How many children do you have?

I have _____ _____ .

3. Do you have sons?

_____ , I _____ .

4. How many sons do you have?

I have _____ _____ .

5. Do you have daughters?

_____ , I _____ .

6. How many daughters do you have?

I have _____ _____ .

City _____

A.   Do you have children?

B.   Yes, I do.

A.   How old are they?

B.   One son is 13.

One daughter is 11.

One daughter is 8.

One son is 2.

A.   Are they in school?

B.   Yes, 3 children are in school.

One child is at home.

Name	How many . . .				
	children	sons	daughters	brothers	sisters

1. How many children do they have?

_____ _____ _____

_____ .

2. How many sons do they have?

_____ _____ _____

_____ .

3. How many daughters do they have?

_____ _____ _____

_____ .

4. How many children does he have?

_____ _____ _____

_____ .

5. How many sons does he have?

_____ _____ _____

_____ .

6. How many daughters does he have?

_____ _____ _____

_____ .

1. How many children does she have?

_____ _____ _____

_____ .

2. How many sons does she have?

_____ _____ _____

_____ .

3. How many daughters does she have?

_____ _____ _____

_____ .

4. How many children do you have?

_____ _____ _____

_____ .

5. How many sons do you have?

_____ _____ _____

_____ .

6. How many daughters do you have?

_____ _____ _____

_____ .

A. Is her son in school?

B. Yes, he is.

A. What school?

B. Bayside Elementary School.

A. What grade?

B. 2nd grade.

A. Who's his teacher?

B. Mrs. Walker.

SCHOOL	AGE
kindergarten	5
1st grade	6
2nd grade	7
3rd grade	8
4th grade	9
5th grade	10
6th grade	11
7th grade	12
8th grade	13
9th grade	14
10th grade	15
11th grade	16
12th grade	17

A. Are you in school?

B. Yes, I am.

A. What school?

B. _____ .

A. Who's your teacher?

B. 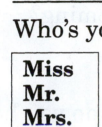 _____

A. Are you a good student?

B. Yes, I am.

---

1. Are you in school?

_____ , _____ _____ .

2. What school? _____ .

3. Who's your teacher? _____ .

A.   Oh, I'm excited.

B.   Why?

A.   Because my family is coming.

B.   Are your brothers and sisters coming?

A.   Yes, they are.

B.   How many brothers and sisters do you have?

A.   I have 2 brothers and 3 sisters.

B.   Are your parents and grandparents coming, too?

A.   Yes, they are.

B.   I'm excited, too.

1. How many brothers do you have?

_____ _____ _____ _____ .

2. How many sisters do you have?

_____ _____ _____ _____ .

3. How many children do you have?

_____ _____ _____ _____ .

4. How many daughters do you have?

_____ _____ _____ _____ .

5. How many sons do you have?

_____ _____ _____ _____ .

6. How many grandchildren do you have?

_____ _____ _____ _____ .

7. How many granddaughters do you have?

_____ _____ _____ _____ .

8. How many grandsons do you have?

_____ _____ _____ _____ .

Irma is excited.

Her family is coming.

Her 3 brothers and 2 sisters are coming.

Her parents are coming too.

---

1. Is Irma excited? _____

2. Is her family coming? _____

3. Are her brothers coming? _____

4. Are her sisters coming? _____

5. Is her friend coming? _____

6. Is her father coming? _____

7. Is her mother coming? _____

1. My name is _____ .

2. I'm from _____ .

3. Now I live in _____ .

4. My address is _____ .

5. My zip code is _____ .

6. My telephone number is _____ .

married	divorced
single	widowed

7. I'm _____ .

8. I have _____ children.

9. I have _____ daughters and _____ sons.

10. _____ children are in school.

11. I go to _____ school.

12. My teacher's name is _____ .

13. This is my family.

My Family   See the Teacher's Guide.

Sue and Kim have 4 children.
They have 2 sons and 2 daughters.
3 children are in school.
1 child is at home.

1. Do Sue and Kim have children?

   _____

2. How many children do they have?

   _____

3. Do they have sons?

   _____

4. How many sons do they have?

   _____

5. Do they have daughters?

   _____

6. How many daughters do they have?

   _____

7. How many children are in school?

   _____

8. How many children are at home?

   _____

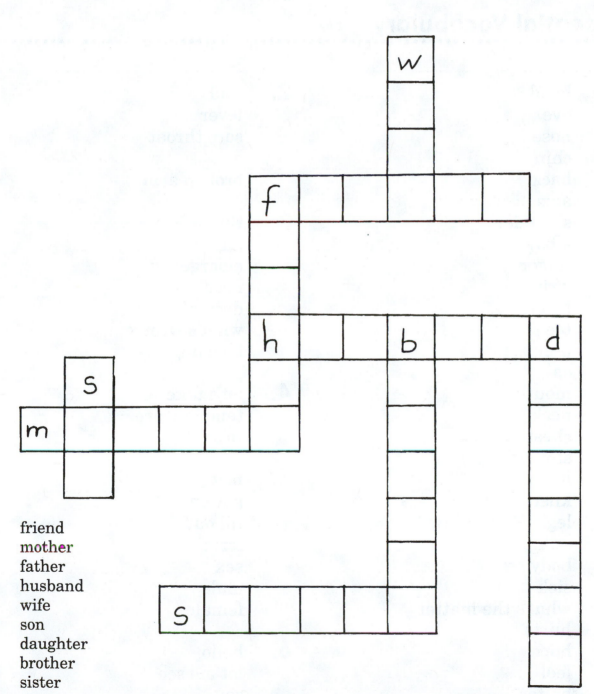

friend
mother
father
husband
wife
son
daughter
brother
sister

4 HEALTH

Essential Vocabulary

··

1. head
eye
nose
chin
back
arm
shoulder
elbow
finger
wrist
foot
toe
hair
ear
mouth
neck
chest
stomach
hand
knee
leg
ankle
body
sick
what's the matter
hurts
hope
feel
better

2. cold
fever
sore throat
a
broken arm

3. this
an
emergency
need
doctor
what's wrong
bleeding

4. let's take
temperature
to see

5. new
patient
fill out
form
sex
male
female

6. hello
let me see
say
cough

some
medicine
here's
prescription
tablet
night
teaspoon
every
hours
drops
capsules

7. Dr. Paul's
office
this
check up
OK
bye

8. coming
dentist
tooth
when
appointment
next

9. hospital
to visit
new
baby
that's wonderful

10. were
had
that's too bad
wrong

THE BODY

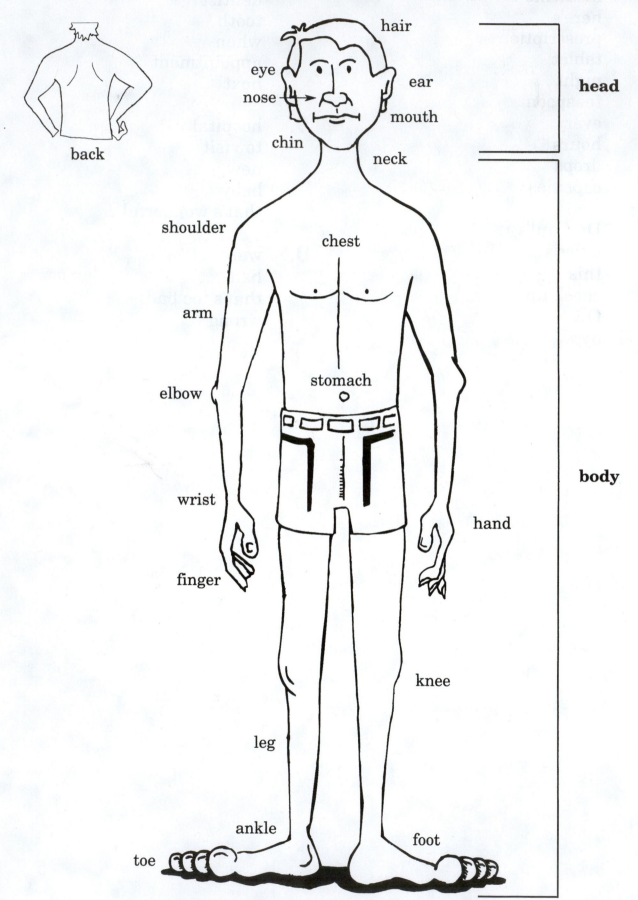

back

hair

eye

ear

nose

mouth

chin

neck

head

shoulder

chest

arm

stomach

elbow

body

wrist

hand

finger

knee

leg

ankle

foot

toe

90

A. How are you?

B. I'm sick.

A. What's the matter?

B. My stomach hurts.

A. I hope you feel better.

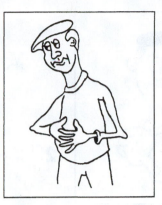

MATCH

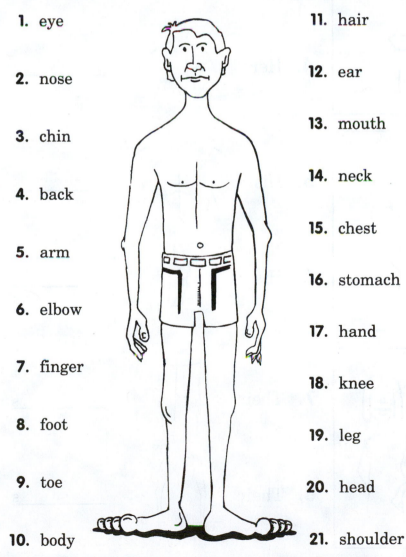

1. eye

2. nose

3. chin

4. back

5. arm

6. elbow

7. finger

8. foot

9. toe

10. body

11. hair

12. ear

13. mouth

14. neck

15. chest

16. stomach

17. hand

18. knee

19. leg

20. head

21. shoulder

WHAT'S THE MATTER?

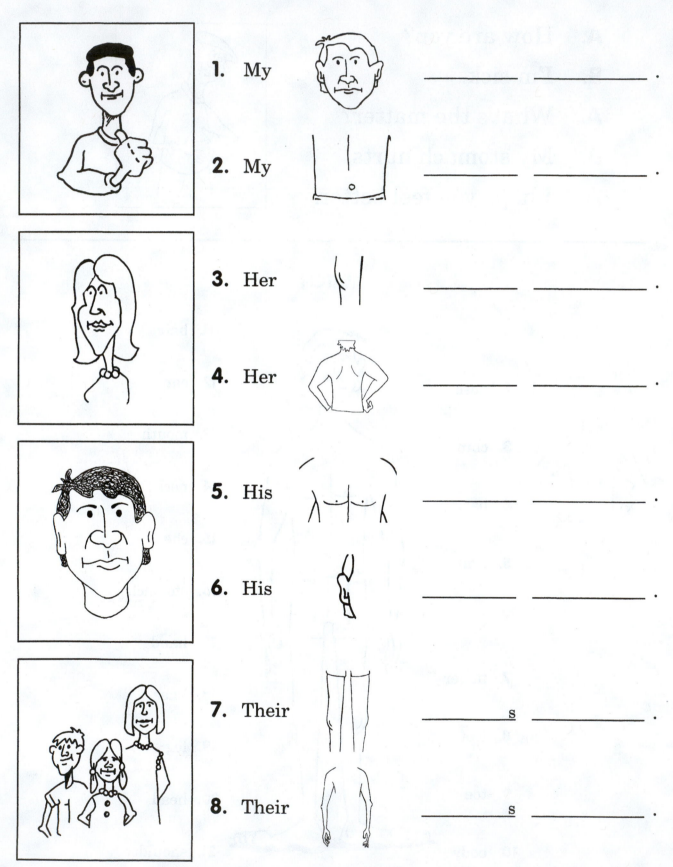

1. My _____ .

2. My _____ .

3. Her _____ .

4. Her _____ .

5. His _____ .

6. His _____ .

7. Their _____s _____ .

8. Their _____s _____ .

A.   Do you have a cold?

B.   Yes, I do.

A.   Do you have a fever?

B.   No, I don't.

1.   They have colds.

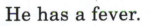

2.   He has a fever.

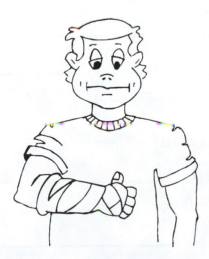

3.   He has a broken arm.

4.   She has a sore throat.

No,	he she	doesn't.	He She	has
	I they	don't.	I They	have

1. Does he have a fever?

No, _____ _____ .

He has _____ _____ _____ .

2. Does she have a cold?

No, _____ _____ .

_____ _____ _____ _____ _____ .

3. Do they have broken arms?

No, _____ _____ .

_____ _____ _____ .

4. Does he have a sore throat?

No, _____ _____ .

_____ _____ _____ _____ .

5. Do you have a cold?

_____ , I _____ .

6. Do you have a fever?

_____ , I _____ .

7. Do you have a sore throat?

_____ , I _____ .

Lee is sick today.
He has a cold.
He has a sore throat.
He isn't going to school.
He's at home.

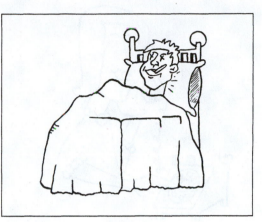

1. How is Lee?

    _____.

2. Is he sick?

    _____.

3. What's the matter?

    _____.

4. Does he have a cold?

    _____.

5. Does he have a sore throat?

    _____.

6. Does his stomach hurt?

    _____.

7. Is he going to school?

    _____.

8. Is he at home?

    _____.

1.

2.

3.

4.

5.

calling
going
filling out

6.

coughing
taking
giving

He's She's	Yes,	he she	is.

1. What's he doing?

_____ _____ .

Is he coughing?

_____ , _____ _____ .

2. What's she doing?

_____ _____ _____ _____ .

Is she calling the doctor?

_____ , _____ _____ .

3. What are they doing?

_____ _____ _____ _____ _____ .

Are they going to the doctor?

_____ , _____ _____ .

4. What's she doing?

_____ _____ _____ _____ .

Is she filling out a form?

_____ , _____ _____ .

5. What's the doctor doing?

_____ _____ _____ .

Is he giving a prescription?

_____ , _____ _____ .

911

A. This is an emergency.

I need a doctor.

B. What's wrong?

A. My daughter's head is bleeding.

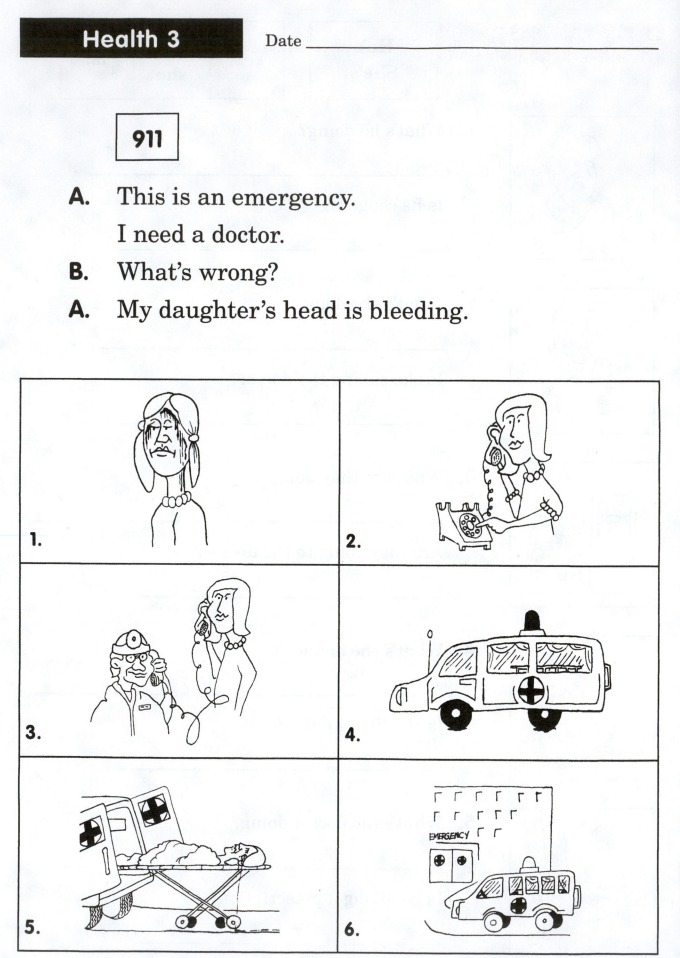

1.

2.

3.

4.

5.

6.

A. What's wrong?

B. I have a sore throat.

A. Let's take your temperature.

It's 104°.

You need to see a doctor.

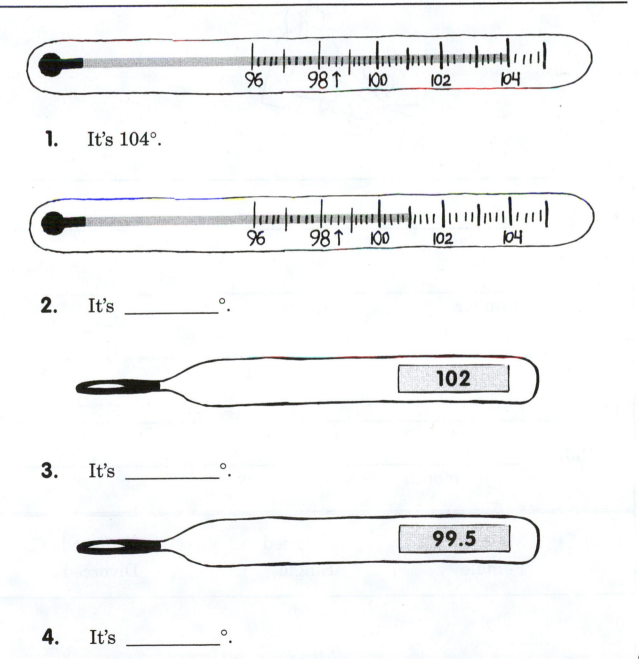

1. It's 104°.

2. It's _____°.

3. It's _____°.

4. It's _____°.

A.   Are you a new patient?

B.   Yes, I am.

A.   Please fill out this form.

Name	_____	_____
	last	first
Address	_____	
	number	street
	_____	
	city	state zip code
Phone	_____ Age	_____
Birthdate	_____	
	month	day year

Sex:	Male ☐	Married ☐	Widowed ☐
	Female ☐	Single ☐	Divorced ☐

A.   Hello.
        What's the matter today?
B.   I have a sore throat.
A.   Let me see.
        Open your mouth.
        Say, "ah."
        Cough.
        You need some medicine.
        Here's a prescription.

1.

2.

3.

Dr. Lee

Name _____   Date _____

Address _____

R̲x

_____
doctor's name

1. How much?

_____

When?

_____

tablespoon

2. How much?

_____

When?

_____

3. How much?

_____

When?

_____

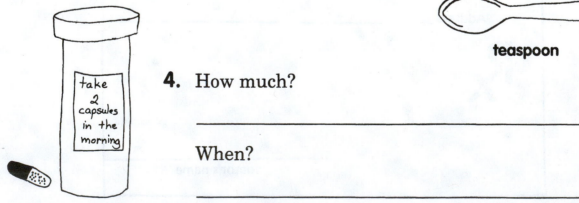

teaspoon

4. How much?

_____

When?

_____

1. How much?

_____

When?

_____

2. How much?

_____

When?

_____

3. How much?

_____

When?

_____

4. How much?

_____

When?

_____

First name _____

A. Hello.

Dr. Paul's office.

B. Hello.

This is _____ .

My son needs a checkup.

A. What's his name?

B. _____ .

A. O.K. Come in tomorrow at 3:00.

B. Thanks, bye.

| need |
| needs |

1. I _____ a checkup.

2. You _____ a checkup.

3. He _____ a checkup.

4. She _____ a checkup.

5. We _____ a checkup.

6. They _____ a checkup.

7. Bob _____ a checkup.

8. Ann _____ a checkup.

WHAT'S THE MATTER?

I	need
he she	needs

1. His head hurts.

He _____ some medicine.

2. Her back hurts.

She _____ some medicine.

3. My stomach hurts.

I _____ some medicine.

4. My ear hurts.

I _____ some medicine.

5. His chest hurts.

He _____ to see a doctor.

6. Her knee hurts.

She _____ to see a doctor.

7. My shoulder hurts.

I _____ to see a doctor.

8. My foot hurts.

I _____ to see a doctor.

medicine

doctor

Telephone number _____

A. Teacher, I'm not coming to school tomorrow.

B. What's wrong?

A. I'm going to the dentist.

B. Does your tooth hurt?

A. No, it doesn't.

I need a checkup.

B. When is your appointment?

A. At 10:00.

B. O.K.

APPOINTMENT

Ann Lee

Mon. Sep. 18   _10:00am_

Marlow L. Toms D.D.S.
792-4836

1. What date is the appointment?

_____

2. What time is the appointment?

_____

NEXT APPOINTMENT

Tue. Jan 4   _4:30 p.m._

Bob Jones

Dr. B. E. White
876-6927

3. What date is the appointment?

_____

4. What time is the appointment?

_____

Zip code _____

A.   Teacher, I'm not coming to school tomorrow.

B.   Why?

A.   Because I'm going to the hospital to visit my friend.

B.   Is she sick?

A.   No, she isn't.
     She has a new baby.

B.   That's wonderful.

DRAW A PERSON

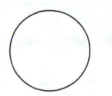

Lila is not coming to school tomorrow.
She is taking her son to the dentist.
Her son has a dentist appointment.
He is not sick.
He has a checkup with the dentist.

---

1. Is Lila coming to school tomorrow?

   _____.

2. Is her son sick?

   _____.

3. Does her son have a toothache?

   _____.

4. Does her son have an appointment?

   _____.

5. Does her son have a checkup?

   _____.

6. Where is the appointment?

   _____.

7. When is the appointment?

   _____.

8. Why does her son have checkups?

   _____.

State _____

A. Were you sick yesterday?

B. Yes, I was.

A. What was wrong?

B. I had a cold.

A. That's too bad.

Yesterday	I he she	was	sick.	Today	I'm he's she's we're you're they're	fine.
	we you they	were				

FILL IN

1. Yesterday I _____ sick. Today _____ fine.

2. Yesterday he _____ sick. Today _____ fine.

3. Yesterday she _____ sick. Today _____ fine.

4. Yesterday we _____ sick. Today _____ fine.

5. Yesterday you _____ sick. Today _____ fine.

6. Yesterday they _____ sick. Today _____ fine.

1. Bob is sick.
He has a fever.

2. His mother calls the doctor.

3. Bob and his mother go to the doctor.

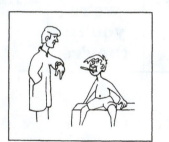

4. The nurse takes Bob's temperature.

5. The doctor gives Bob a prescription.

The nurse takes Bob's temperature.

His mother calls the doctor.

Bob is sick. He has a fever.

Bob and his mother go to the doctor.

The doctor gives Bob a prescription.

See the Teacher's Guide.

Yesterday	I you we they he she it	had	medicine.

Today	I you we they	have	medicine.
	he she it	has	

FILL IN

1. Yesterday I _____ a cold.

2. Today I _____ a cough.

3. Yesterday he _____ a toothache.

4. Today he _____ a dentist appointment.

5. Yesterday she _____ a temperature.

6. Now she _____ a headache.

7. I _____ a fever yesterday.

8. Now I _____ some medicine.

9. Yesterday they _____ sore throats.

10. Today they _____ checkups.

Tran was sick yesterday.
He wasn't at school.
He had a sore throat.

---

1. Who was sick yesterday?

_____.

2. Was Tran sick yesterday?

_____.

3. Was Tran at home yesterday?

_____.

4. Was Tran at school yesterday?

_____.

5. What was wrong?

_____.

6. Why was Tran home?

_____.

7. Were you sick yesterday?

_____.

8. Were you at school yesterday?

_____.

9. Were you at home yesterday?

_____.

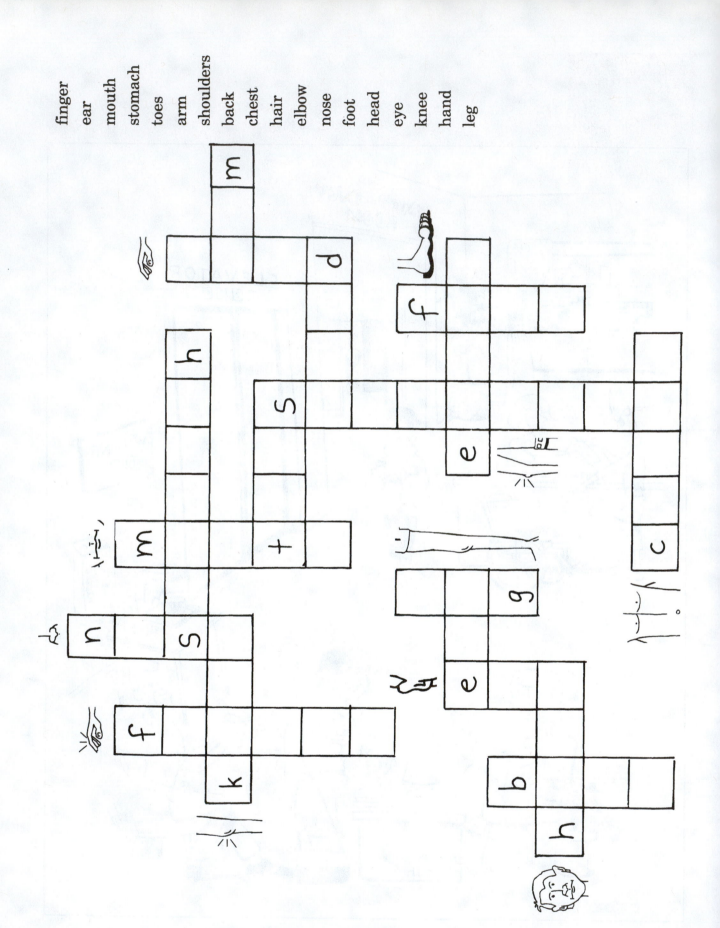

finger ear mouth stomach toes arm shoulders back chest hair elbow nose foot head eye knee hand leg

114

5 TRANSPORTATION

Essential Vocabulary
....

1. drive
take
train
ride

2. Bus Company
downtown
to transfer
every hour

3. bus stop
over there
in front of
in back of
next to
gas station

4. how much
one way

5. watch your step
be careful

6. grocery store
First Street
on the corner
pharmacy

7. lost
shopping center
turn left
turn right
block

8. driver's license
I'm sorry

9. too fast
speed limit
giving
ticket

10. mechanic
check
car
sure
engine
battery
radiator
just
water
trunk

1.

2.

3.

4.

5.

6.

7.

8.

9.

bicycle
van
bus

motorcycle
boat
airplane

car / truck
subway
train

City _____

A. I drive to school.

How do you go to school?

B. I take the bus.

I drive a

1.

2.

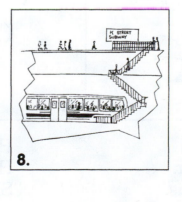
3.

I ride a   to school.

4.

5.

6.

I take the

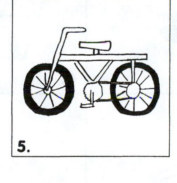
7.

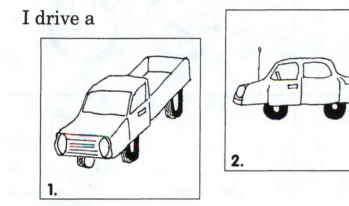
8.

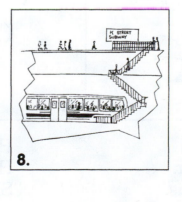
9.

117

How does $\boxed{\begin{array}{c}\textbf{he}\\\textbf{she}\end{array}}$ go?

1.

2.

3.

4.

5.

6.

She walks.
He drives his car.
She takes the bus.

He rides his bicycle.
He takes the subway.
She takes an airplane.

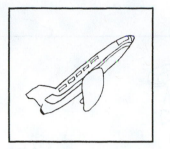

1. How does she go to L.A.?

She _____ _____ _____.

Does she take an airplane?

Yes, _____ _____.

2. How does he go to L.A.?

He _____ _____ _____.

Does he drive a car?

Yes, _____ _____.

3. How does he go to L.A.?

He _____ _____ _____.

Does he take the train?

Yes, _____ _____.

4. How does he go to school?

He _____ _____ _____.

Does he ride his bicycle?

Yes, _____ _____.

5. How does she go to school?

She _____ _____ _____.

Does she take the bus?

Yes, _____ _____.

6. How does she go to school?

She _____.

Does she walk to school?

Yes, _____ _____.

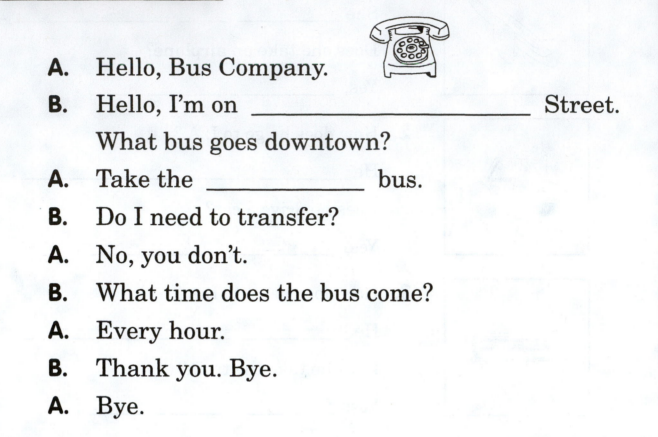

A. Hello, Bus Company.

B. Hello, I'm on _____ Street. What bus goes downtown?

A. Take the _____ bus.

B. Do I need to transfer?

A. No, you don't.

B. What time does the bus come?

A. Every hour.

B. Thank you. Bye.

A. Bye.

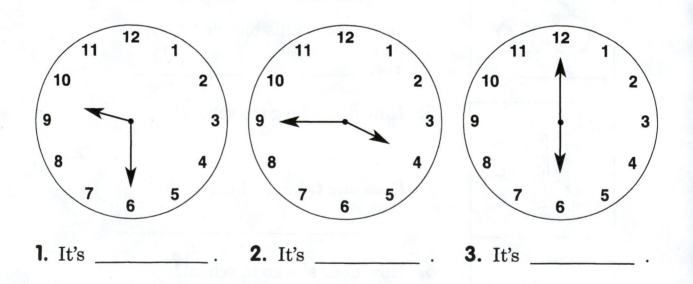

1. It's _____ .   **2.** It's _____ .   **3.** It's _____ .

Who?	How do they come to school? How does [he/she] come to school?	How do they go downtown? How does [he/she] go downtown?
1. 		
2.		
3.		

See the Teacher's Guide.

1.

2.

3.

4.

5.

6.

7.

8.

9.

10.

11.

12.

downtown
grocery store
laundromat
shopping center

hospital
home
park
theater

school
church / temple
pharmacy
gas station

A. Where's the bus stop?

B. It's over there.

It's ┌─────────────┐ the gas station.
│ **in front of** │
│ **in back of** │
│ **next to** │
└─────────────┘

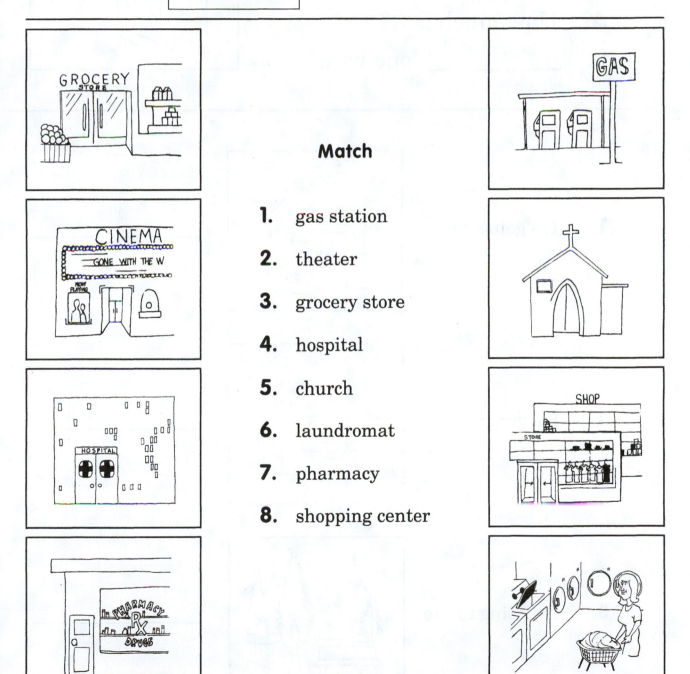

Match

1. gas station

2. theater

3. grocery store

4. hospital

5. church

6. laundromat

7. pharmacy

8. shopping center

Birth date _____

A. Where are you going?

B. I'm going downtown.

A. Are you taking the bus?

B. Yes, I am.

A. How much is it?

B. _____ one way.

---

1. I'm going 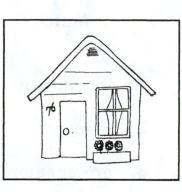 _____.

2. I'm going to  _____.

3. I'm going to the  _____.

Age _____

A. Is this bus going downtown?

B. Yes, it is. Watch your step. Be careful.

A. Do I need to transfer?

B. No, you don't.

A. Thanks.

Do	I you we they	_____ ?

Does	he she	_____ ?

1. _____ I need to transfer?

2. _____ they need to transfer?

3. _____ we need to transfer?

4. _____ she need to _____ ?

5. _____ he need to _____ ?

6. _____ I need _____ _____ ?

7. _____ you need _____ _____ ?

8. _____ they _____ _____ _____ ?

9. _____ she _____ _____ _____ ?

10. _____ he _____ _____ _____ ?

Where's the _____ **going?**

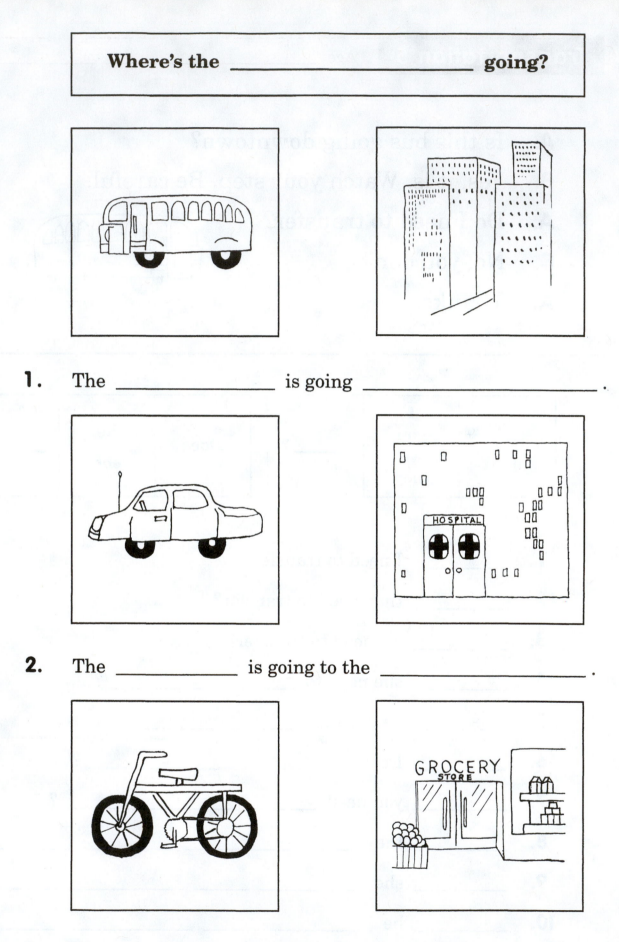

1. The _____ is going _____.

2. The _____ is going to the _____.

3. The _____ is going to the _____ _____.

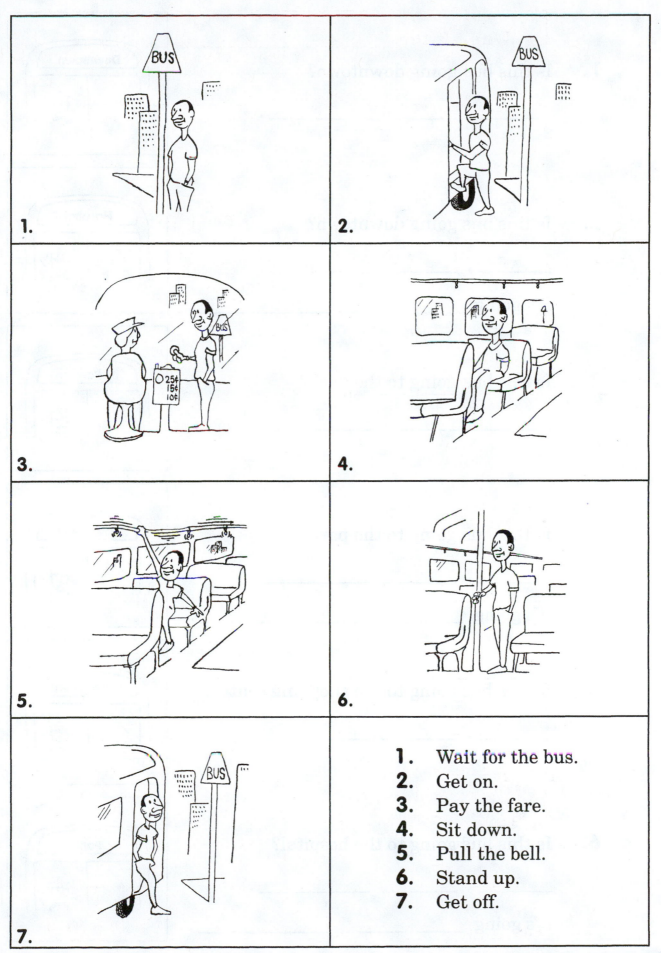

1. Wait for the bus.
2. Get on.
3. Pay the fare.
4. Sit down.
5. Pull the bell.
6. Stand up.
7. Get off.

See the Teacher's Guide.

1. Is this bus going downtown?

   _____ , _____ _____ .

2. Is this bus going downtown?

   _____ , _____ _____ .

   It's going _____ _____ _____ .

3. Is this bus going to the park?

   _____ , _____ _____ .

4. Is this bus going to the park?

   _____ , _____ _____ .

   It's going _____ .

5. Is this bus going to the shopping center?

   _____ , _____ _____ .

6. Is this bus going to the hospital?

   _____ , _____ _____ .

   It's going _____ _____ _____ .

A.   Excuse me. Where's the grocery store?

B.   It's on First Street.

A.   Is it on the corner?

B.   No, it isn't. It's next to the pharmacy.

A.   Thank you.

Where's the _____ ? It's

next to in front of	the _____.
on the corner.	
across the street.	

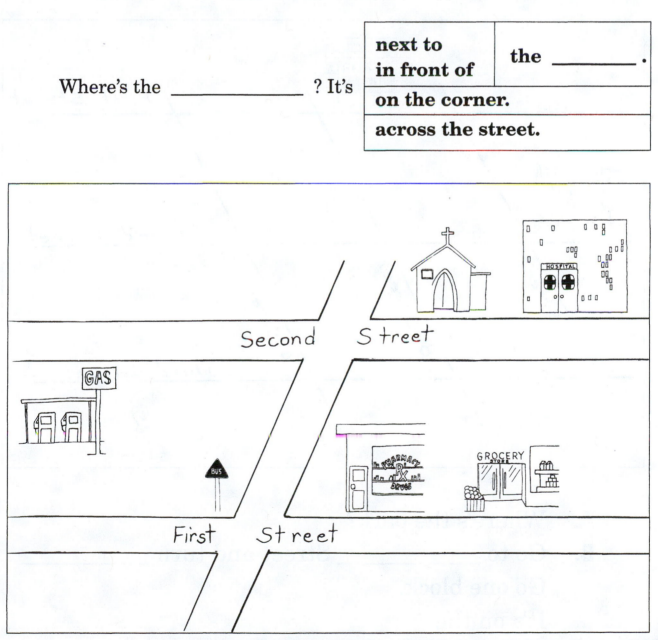

A. I'm lost. Where's the shopping center?

B. Go to A Street and turn right.
Turn left on First Street.
Turn right on B Street.
It's on the corner.

A. Thanks.

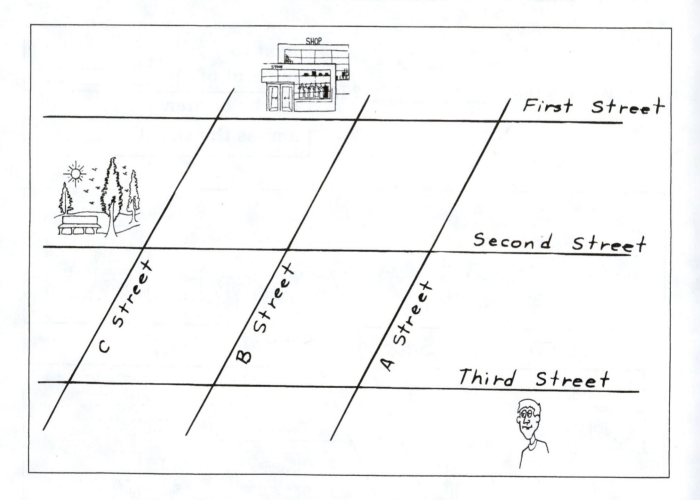

A. Where's the park?

B. Go to _____ Street and turn _____ .
Go one block.
It's on the _____ .

MAP

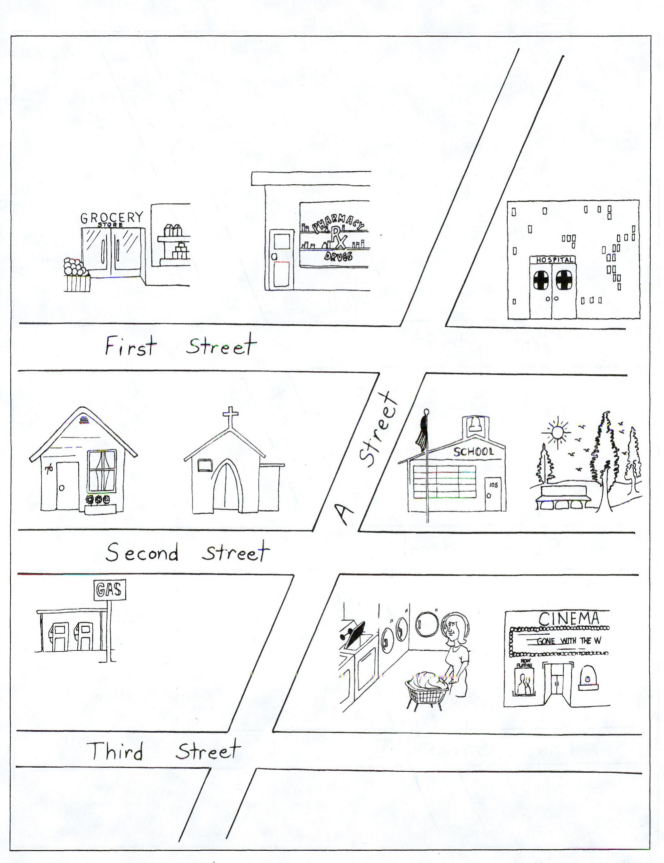

First Street

A Street

Second Street

Third Street

GROCERY STORE

PHARMACY RX DRUGS

HOSPITAL

GAS

SCHOOL

CINEMA
GONE WITH THE W

See the Teacher's Guide.

MAP

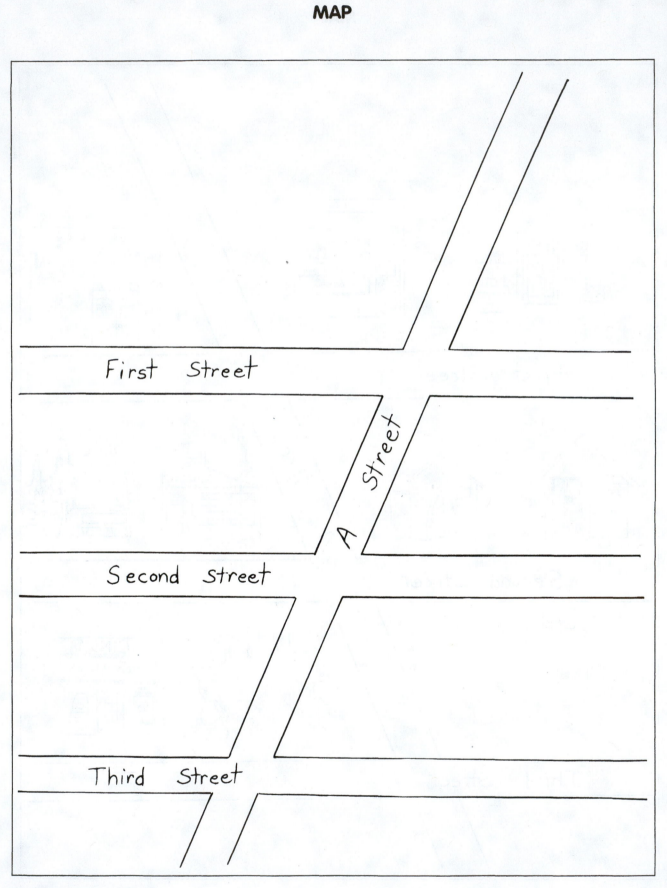

First Street

A Street

Second Street

Third Street

1. **Where's the pharmacy?**

   It's _____ on _____ First _____ Street. _____

   Is it on the corner?

   _____ , _____ _____ .

2. **Where's the laundromat?**

   It's _____ _____ _____ .

   Is it on the corner?

   _____ , _____ _____ .

3. **Where's the church?**

   It's _____ _____ _____ .

   Is it on the corner?

   _____ , _____ _____ .

4. **Where's the park?**

   It's _____ _____ _____ .

   Is it on the corner?

   _____ , _____ _____ .

5. **Where's the grocery store?**

   It's _____ _____ _____ .

   Is it on the corner?

   _____ , _____ _____ .

6. **Where's the hospital?**

   It's _____ _____ _____ .

   Is it on the corner?

   _____ , _____ _____ .

Who?	Where?	How?

1.

2.

3.

See the Teacher's Guide.

First name _____

A. Do you have a driver's license?

B. No, I don't.

A. That's too bad.

You need a driver's license.

B. Oh, I'm sorry.

A. Don't drive.

B. Don't drive?

A. Don't drive!

B. O.K.

---

1.  Don't turn left.

2.  No left turn.

3.  Don't walk.
No walking.

4.  Don't turn right.

5.  No right turn.

6.  Don't make a U-turn.

7. No U-turn.

Mary is going to a movie.
The theater is downtown.
She takes the #10 bus.
She doesn't need to transfer.
The fare is $1.25 one way.

---

1. Who's going to the movie?

_____

2. Where's Mary going?

_____

3. Where's the theater?

_____

4. Is Mary going to a movie?

_____

5. Is Mary going downtown?

_____

6. Is Mary taking the bus?

_____

7. Is Mary driving a car?

_____

8. What bus goes downtown?

_____

9. How much is the fare one way?

_____

10. How much is the fare round trip?

_____

A. Do you have a driver's license?

B. Yes, I do. What's the matter?

A. You were driving too fast. The speed limit is 55, not 65.

B. I'm sorry.

A. I'm giving you a ticket.

1.

2.

3.

4.

5.

6.

7.

8.

9.

A. Are you a mechanic?

B. Yes, I am.

A. Can you check my car?

B. Sure.

A. How's the engine?

B. It's OK.

A. How's the battery?

B. It's OK.

A. How's the radiator?

B. It just needs some water.

A. Oh, good. Thanks.

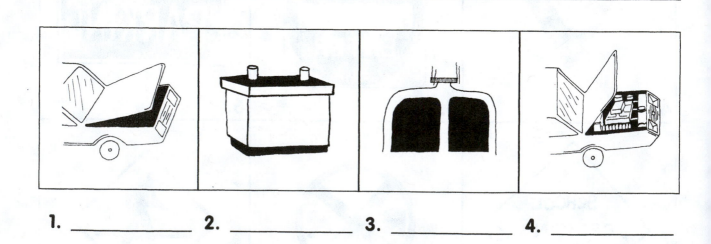

1. _____   2. _____   3. _____   4. _____

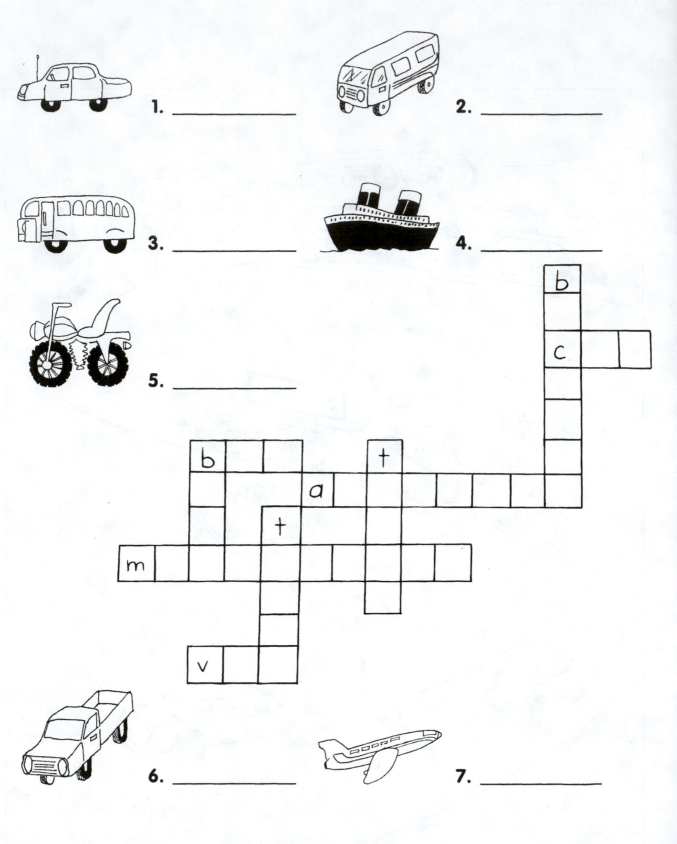

1. _____

2. _____

3. _____

4. _____

5. _____

6. _____

7. _____

8. _____

9. _____

Essential Vocabulary
....

1.   bread
   and
   eggs
   milk
   ice cream

2.   hot dogs
   hamburger
   buy some
   pound
   one sale

3.   broccoli
   celery
   onions
   pineapple
   pears
   oranges
   mushrooms
   bananas
   grapes
   ea.
   lb.

4.   to return
   meat
   fresh
   you're right
   receipt

5.   hungry
   let's eat
   like

6.   to make
   cake
   cake mix
   cup
   oil
   turn on
   oven
   grease
   pan
   flour
   put
   mix
   bowl
   add
   stir
   wait
   minutes

7.   next
   colas
   small
   medium
   large
   to go

1.	2.	3.	4.
5.	6.	7.	8.
9.	10.	11.	12.
13.	14.	15.	16.

bread	hot dog	fish	rice
eggs	a hamburger	chicken	oil
milk	soda pop	pork	tea
ice cream	coffee	hamburger	cake mix

A.   I'm going to the store.

What do you need?

B.   I need bread and eggs.

A.   Do you need milk?

B.   No. I don't. I have milk.

A.   Do you want ice cream?

B.   No, I don't.

	have / has	need / needs
I You They We		
He She		

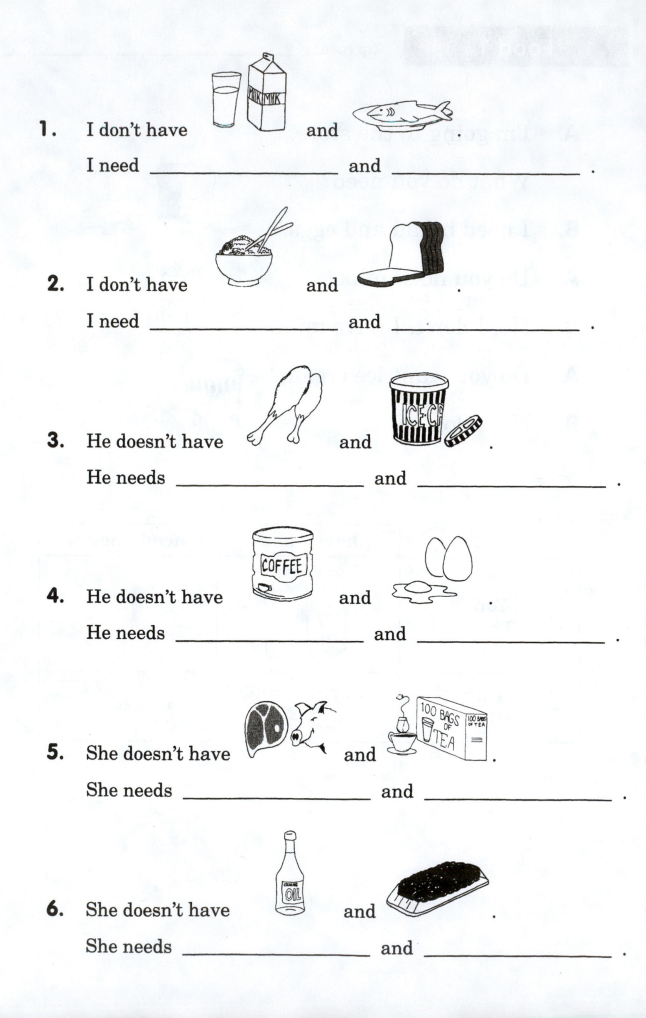

1. I don't have _____ and _____

   I need _____ and _____ .

2. I don't have _____ and _____ .

   I need _____ and _____ .

3. He doesn't have _____ and _____ .

   He needs _____ and _____ .

4. He doesn't have _____ and _____ .

   He needs _____ and _____ .

5. She doesn't have _____ and _____ .

   She needs _____ and _____ .

6. She doesn't have _____ and _____ .

   She needs _____ and _____ .

State _____

pound — lb.

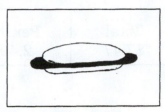

A. Do you like hot dogs?

B. No, I don't.

A. Do you like hamburger?

B. Yes, I do. I want to buy some.

A. It's $1.09 on sale.

Hamburger		
Per lb. $1.89	Total $5.67	Wt. 3 lbs.
J. G.'s Market		

How much is it a pound?

_____

What's the total?

_____

Pork		
Total $7.47	Per lb. 2.49	Wt. 3 lbs.

1. How much is it a pound?

   _____

2. What's the total?

   _____

FISH MARKET		
Wt. 2.5 lbs.	Total $11.88	Per lb. $4.75
Fish		

3. How much is it a pound?

   _____

4. What's the total?

   _____

Hamburger		
Per lb. $1.96	Total $6.94	Wt. 3.54 lbs.

5. How much is it a pound?

   _____

6. What's the total?

   _____

QUACKY FARMS		
Per lb. $0.99	Wt. 5.62 lbs.	Total $5.57
Chicken		

7. How much is it a pound?

   _____

8. What's the total?

   _____

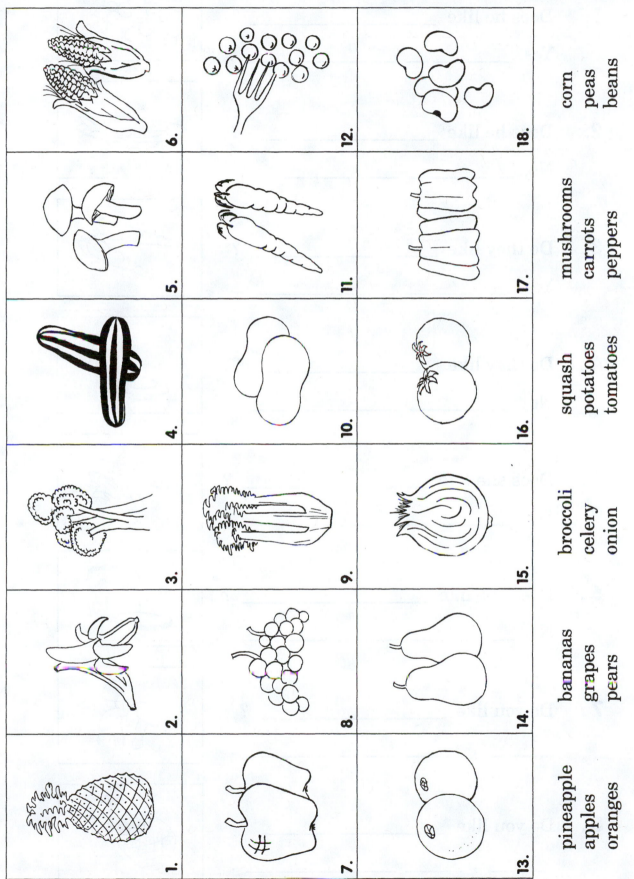

1.

2. bananas
   grapes
   pears

3. broccoli
   celery
   onion

4. squash
   potatoes
   tomatoes

5. mushrooms
   carrots
   peppers

6. corn
   peas
   beans

7.

8.

9.

10.

11.

12.

13. pineapple
    apples
    oranges

14.

15.

16.

17.

18.

pineapple
apples
oranges

bananas
grapes
pears

broccoli
celery
onion

squash
potatoes
tomatoes

mushrooms
carrots
peppers

corn
peas
beans

1. Does he like _____ ?

   Yes, _____ _____ .

2. Does he like _____ ?

   No, _____ _____ .

3. Do they like _____ ?

   Yes, _____ _____ .

4. Do they like _____ ?

   No, _____ _____ .

5. Does she like _____ ?

   Yes, _____ _____ .

6. Does she like _____ ?

   No, _____ _____ .

7. Do you like _____ ?

   _____ , _____ _____ .

8. Do you like _____ ?

   _____ , _____ _____ .

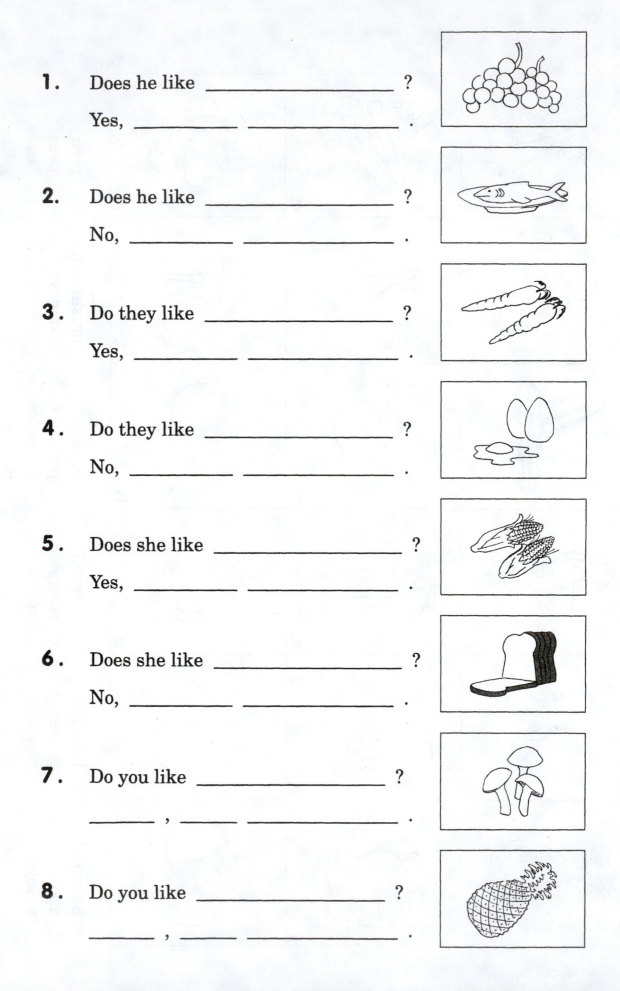

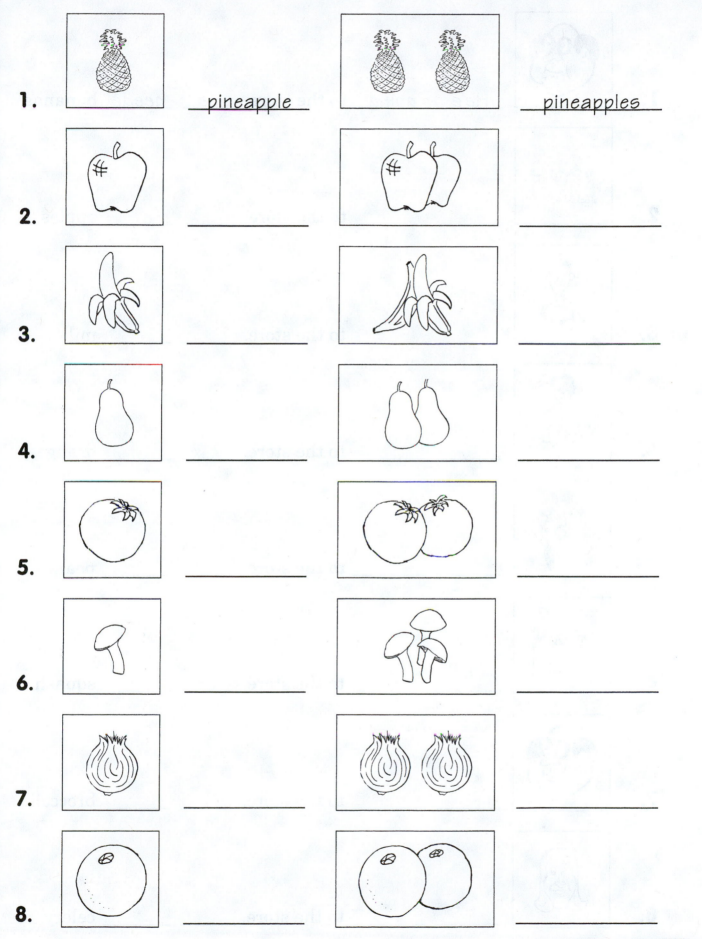

1. pineapple   pineapples

2.

3.

4.

5.

6.

7.

8.

149

1. _He's_ _going_ to the store. _He_ _needs_ bananas.

2. _____ _____ to the store. _____ _____ apples.

3. _____ _____ to the store. _____ _____ milk.

4. _____ _____ to the store. _____ _____ oranges.

5. _____ _____ to the store. _____ _____ pears.

6. _____ _____ to the store. _____ _____ squash.

7. _____ _____ to the store. _____ _____ broccoli.

8. _____ _____ to the store. _____ _____ celery.

A. How much is the  ?

B. 89¢ a lb.

A. How much is the  ?

B. 79¢ ea.

A. How much are the  ?

B. 42¢ a lb.

A. How much is the  ?

B. $3.10 ea.

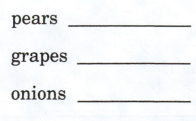

$1.05 a lb.

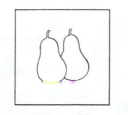

59¢ a lb.

49¢ a lb.

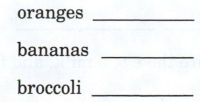

$1.98 ½ lb.

87¢ a lb.

55¢ a lb.

pears _____   oranges _____   pineapple _____

grapes _____   bananas _____   mushrooms _____

onions _____   broccoli _____   celery _____

$1.50 a doz.

$1.02

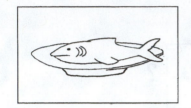

$2.17 ea.

78¢ a lb.

1. How much is the fish?

    It's _____ .

2. How much is the milk?

    It's _____ .

3. How much are the eggs?

    They're _____ .

4. How much are the oranges?

    They're _____ .

5. How much are the fish and eggs?

    _____ _____ .

6. How much are the milk and eggs?

    _____ _____ .

7. How much are the milk and fish?

    _____ _____ .

8. How much are the eggs, milk, and fish?

    _____ _____ .

Keo is going to the grocery store. He needs eggs, rice, and oranges. He has bananas and milk.

1. Who's going to the grocery store?

   _____.

2. Where's Keo going?

   _____.

3. Is he going to the grocery store?

   _____.

4. What does Keo need?

   _____.

5. What does Keo have?

   _____.

6. Does Keo need eggs?

   _____.

7. Does Keo need rice?

   _____.

8. Does Keo need milk?

   _____.

9. Does Keo have bananas?

   _____.

10. Does Keo have milk?

    _____.

11. Does Keo need bananas?

    _____.

A.   Excuse me. I want to return this meat.

B.   Why?

A.   Because it isn't fresh.

B.   Let me see. Oh! You're right.
     Do you have the receipt?

A.   Yes, I do.

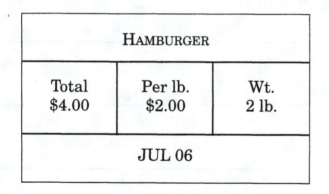

HAMBURGER		
Total $4.00	Per lb. $2.00	Wt. 2 lb.
JUL 06		

Today is July 6.

1. What's the date on the meat?

_____

2. Is it fresh?

_____ , _____ _____ .

Today is November 15.

3. What's the date on the milk?

_____

4. Is it fresh?

_____ , _____ _____ .

154

1.

2.

3.

4.

5.
eating
returning
shopping

6.
drinking
making / cooking
buying

155

1. What's he doing?

_____ _____ .

Is he eating?

_____ , _____ _____ .

2. What's she doing?

_____ _____ .

Is she shoppng?

_____ , _____ _____ .

3. What's he doing?

_____ .

Is he eating?

_____ , _____ _____ .

4. What's she doing?

_____ _____ meat.

Is she cooking?

_____ , _____ _____ .

5. What's he doing?

_____ .

Is he drinking?

_____ , _____ _____ .

6. What's she doing?

_____ _____ food.

Is she returning meat?

_____ , _____ _____ .

Soc. Sec. No. _____

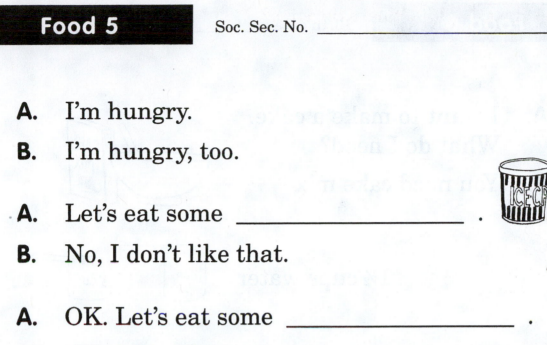

A. I'm hungry.

B. I'm hungry, too.

A. Let's eat some _____ .

B. No, I don't like that.

A. OK. Let's eat some _____ .

B. OK. I like them.

He's hungry.
He's eating a hot dog.

He's thirsty.
He's drinking.

157

A. I want to make a cake.
What do I need?

B. You need cake mix

1½ cups water

⅓ cup oil

and 3 eggs.

A. Do you want to help?

B. Sure.

A. 1. Turn on the oven to 350°.
   2. Grease the pan.
   3. Flour the pan.
   4. Put the mix in the bowl.
   5. Add the water.
   6. Add the eggs.
   7. Add the oil.
   8. Stir it up.
   9. Put the mix in the pan.
  10. Put the pan in the oven.
  11. Wait 35 minutes.
  12. Take the pan out of the oven.

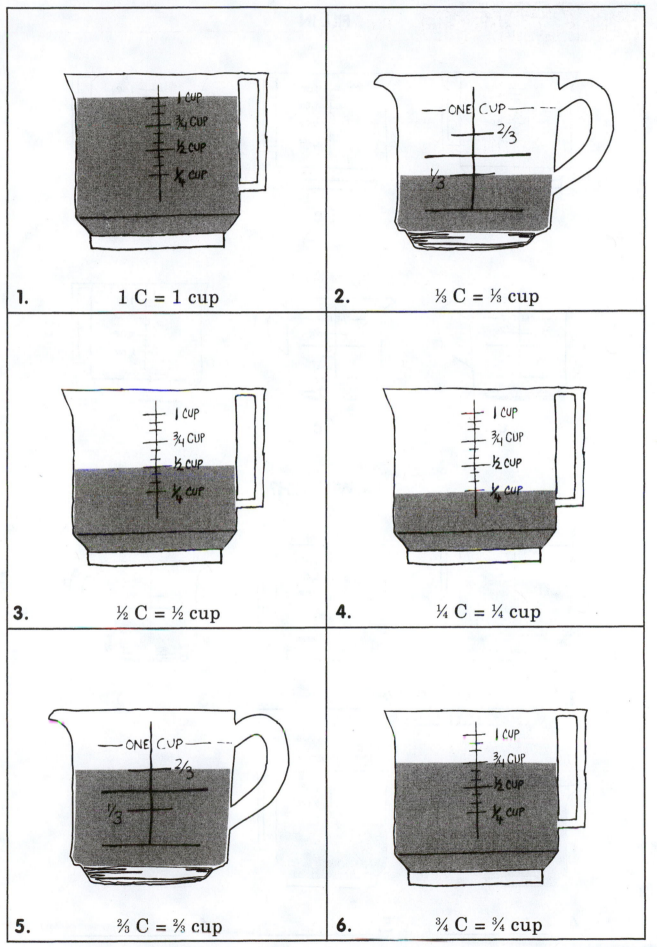

1. 1 C = 1 cup

2. ⅓ C = ⅓ cup

3. ½ C = ½ cup

4. ¼ C = ¼ cup

5. ⅔ C = ⅔ cup

6. ¾ C = ¾ cup

FILL IN

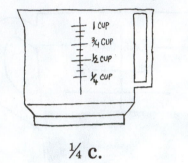

¼ c.

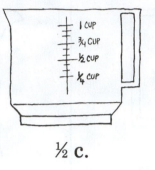

½ c.

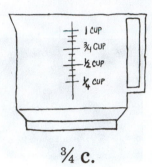

¾ c.

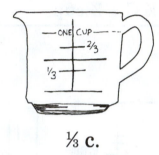

⅓ c.

⅔ c.

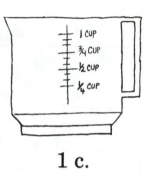

1 c.

HOW MUCH?

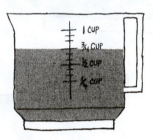

1. _____

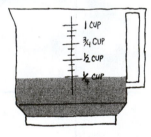

2. _____

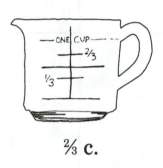

3. _____

4. _____

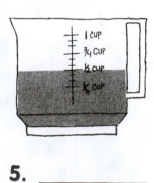

5. _____

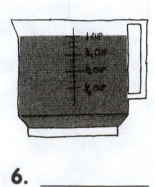

6. _____

Powdered Milk

1⅓ C powdered milk mix

4 C water

mix

1. How much water? _____

2. How much powdered milk mix? _____

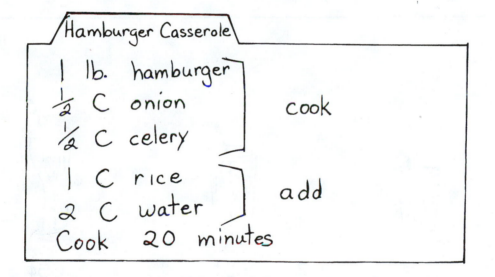

Hamburger Casserole

1 lb. hamburger
½ C onion   } cook
½ C celery

1 C rice   } add
2 C water
Cook 20 minutes

3. How much water? _____

4. How much onion? _____

5. How much hamburger? _____

6. How much celery? _____

7. How much rice? _____

A. Next, please.

B. I want two colas.

A. Small, medium, or large?

B. One small, one medium.

A. Is that for here or to go?

B. To go.

A. That's $1.00.

1. ___45¢___

2. ___55¢___

3. ___65¢___

4. ___65¢___   5. ___95¢___   6. ___60¢___   7. ___90¢___

Julia cooks every day. Today she opens the hamburger. It isn't fresh. She needs fresh hamburger. She has the receipt. She's going to the grocery store now.

1. Who cooks every day?

   _____ .

2. Is the hamburger fresh?

   _____ .

3. Does she need fresh hamburger?

   _____ .

4. Does she want to return it?

   _____ .

5. Does she have the receipt?

   _____ .

6. Where is Julia going now?

   _____ .

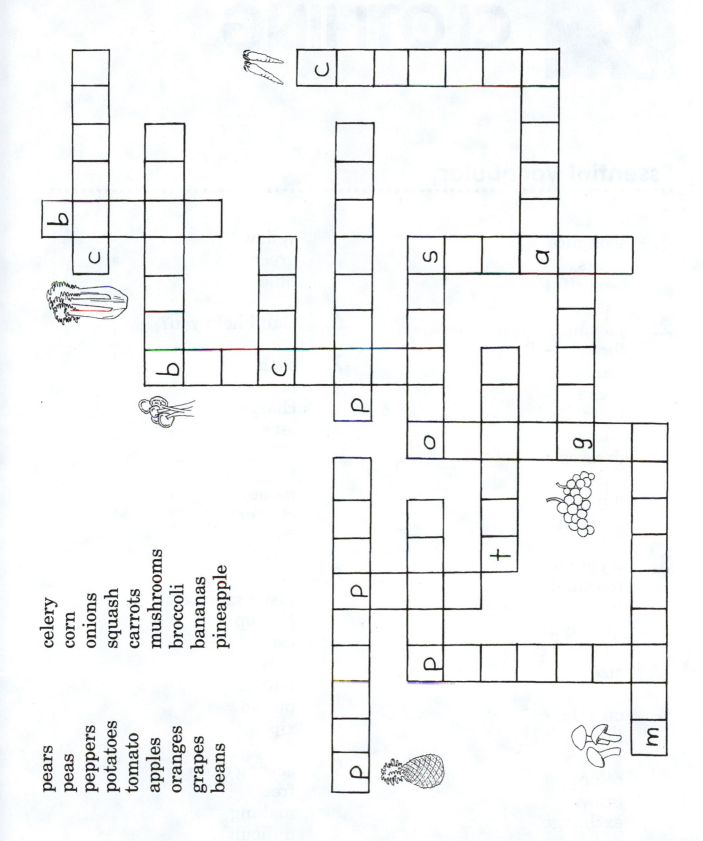

pears
peas
peppers
potatoes
tomato
apples
oranges
grapes
beans

celery
corn
onions
squash
carrots
mushrooms
broccoli
bananas
pineapple

 **CLOTHING**

Essential Vocabulary
....

1. look nice
dress
beautiful

2. jackets
for
pants
socks
belts
shoes
dresses
shirts
hats
sweaters

3. try it on
too small
too big
just right
let's buy it
size

4. on sale
I'll buy it

5. color
brown
exchange
red
black

yellow
green
blue

6. Can I help you?

7. cash
or
charge
let's see
plus
tax
money
change
from

8. outside
just a minute
pull up
tie
now
button
put on
zip

9. sewing class
free
making
difficult
easy
fun

10. pick up
thread
scissors
cut
needle
knot
material
sew
up
down

11. laundromat
clothes
to wash
soap
bleach
machines

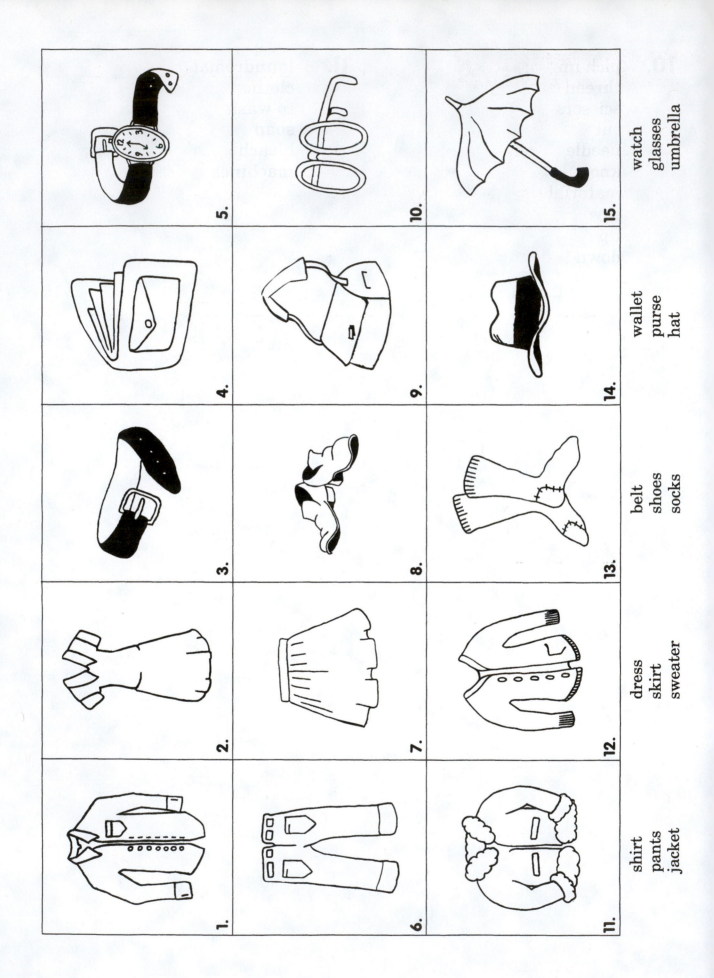

shirt
pants
jacket

dress
skirt
sweater

belt
shoes
socks

wallet
purse
hat

watch
glasses
umbrella

1.

2.

3.

4.

5.

6.

7.

8.

9.

10.

11.

12.

13.

14.

15.

Signature _____

A. You look nice today.
Is that a new dress?
B. Yes, it is.
A. It's beautiful.
B. Thank you.

1. _____

2. _____

3. _____

4. _____

5. _____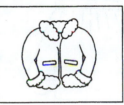

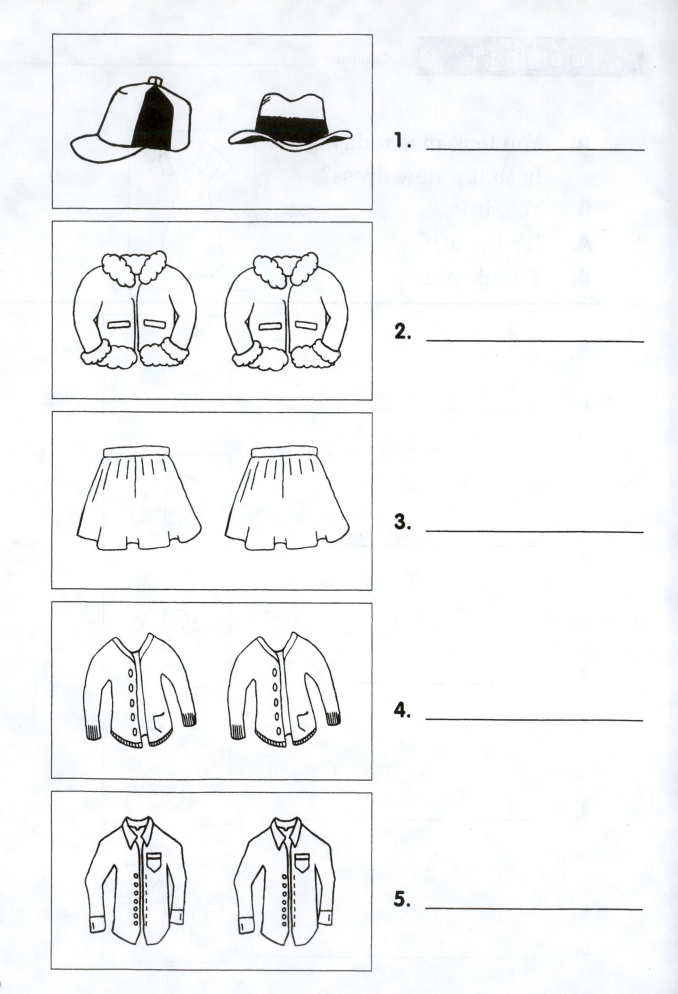

1. _____

2. _____

3. _____

4. _____

5. _____

A.   I'm going to the shopping center.

B.   When?

A.   At 2:00. Do you want to come?

B.   Yes, I do. I need to buy jackets for my children.

---

1.   I   need   to   buy   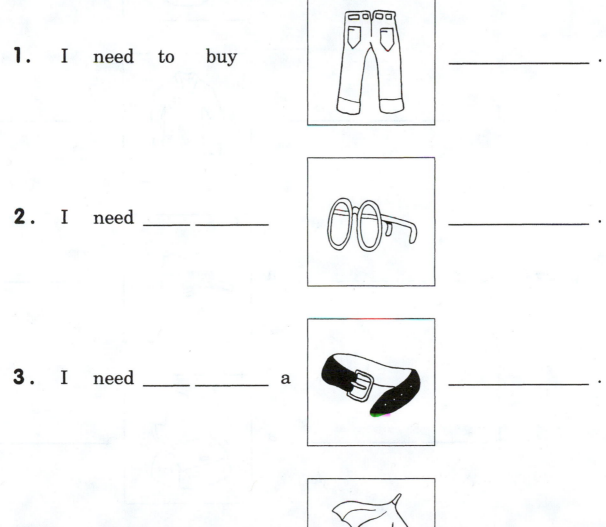 _____ .

2.   I   need _____ _____ _____ .

3.   I   need _____ _____ a _____ .

4.   I   need _____ _____ an  _____ .

1. I _____ a 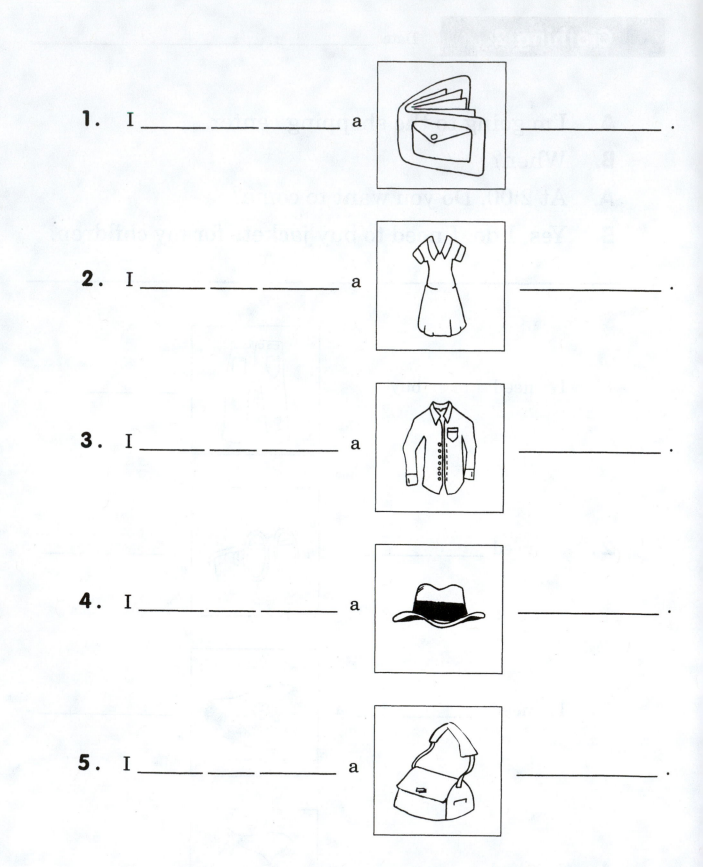 _____ .

2. I _____ a _____ .

3. I _____ a _____ .

4. I _____ a _____ .

5. I _____ a _____ .

A. Here's a jacket. Try it on.
B. It's too small.

A. Try this one.
B. It's too big.

A. Well, try this one.
B. It's just right.
A. OK. Let's buy it.

WHAT SIZE IS IT?

Small, medium, or large? Write the answer on each blank.

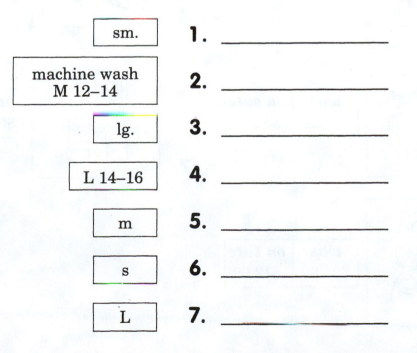

sm.	**1.** _____
machine wash M 12–14	**2.** _____
lg.	**3.** _____
L 14–16	**4.** _____
m	**5.** _____
s	**6.** _____
L	**7.** _____

A.   I like this dress.
      How much is it?
B.   Now it's $26.00 on sale.
A.   On sale?
B.   Yes, it was $35.00.
A.   I'll buy it.

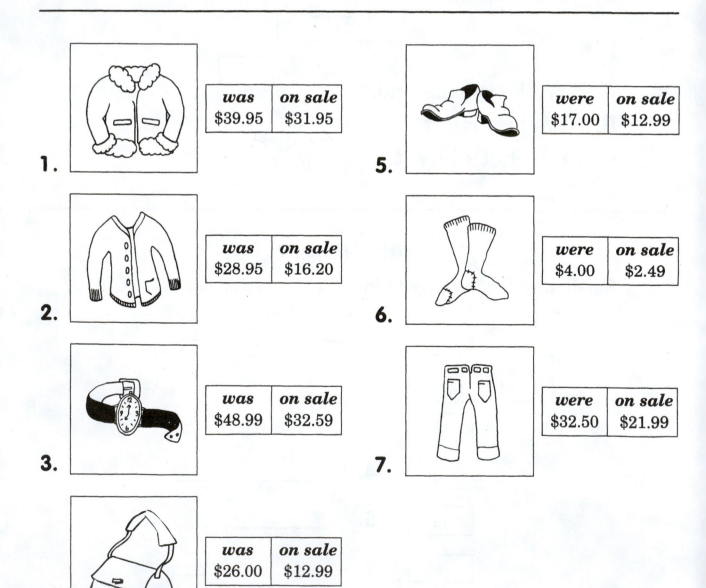

	was	*on sale*
1.	$39.95	$31.95

	was	*on sale*
2.	$28.95	$16.20

	was	*on sale*
3.	$48.99	$32.59

	was	*on sale*
4.	$26.00	$12.99

	were	*on sale*
5.	$17.00	$12.99

	were	*on sale*
6.	$4.00	$2.49

	were	*on sale*
7.	$32.50	$21.99

ON SALE

$16.99 $8.49 $21.00

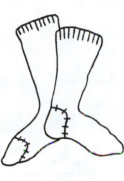

$1.99 $11.99 $15.00

1. How much is the sweater? _____ .

2. How much are the socks? _____ .

3. How much is the skirt? _____ .

4. How much are the pants? _____ .

5. How much is the shirt? _____ .

6. How much are the shoes? _____ .

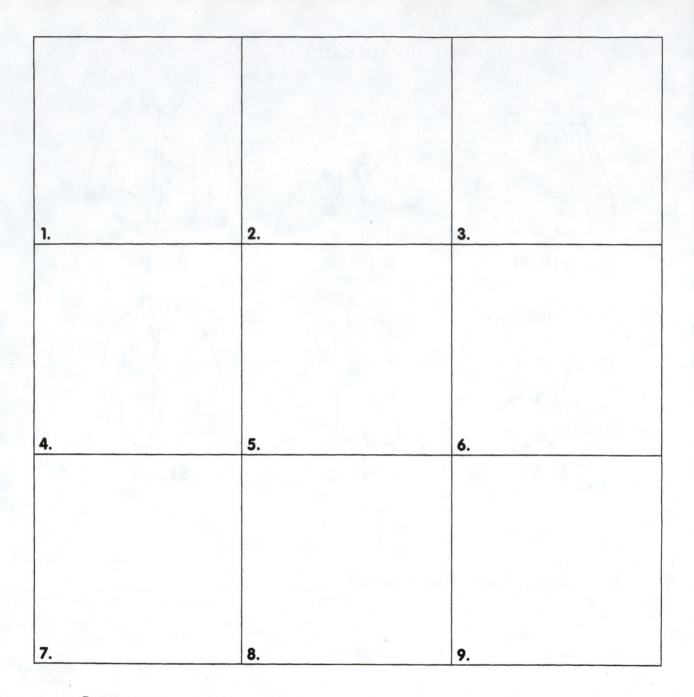

1.   Color number 1 red.
2.   Color number 2 green.
3.   Color number 3 yellow.
4.   Color number 4 orange.
5.   Color number 5 blue.
6.   Color number 6 purple.
7.   Color number 7 brown.
8.   Color number 8 black.
9.   Don't color number 9. It's white.

See the Teacher's Guide.

Ann needs to buy jackets for her children. She needs 1 small and 1 large jacket. The children want blue jackets. Ann wants to buy the jackets on sale.

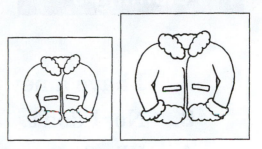

1. Does Ann need jackets for her children?

   _____.

2. How many jackets does she need?

   _____.

3. What colors?

   _____.

4. What sizes?

   _____.

5. Does she want to buy the jackets on sale?

   _____.

6. Do the children want blue jackets?

   _____.

7. Do the children want yellow jackets?

   _____.

8. Do you have a jacket?

   _____.

9. What color is it?

   _____.

10. What size is it?

   _____.

A. I have a new dress. Do you like it?

B. No, I don't.

A. Why?

B. Because I don't like the color.
    I don't like brown.

A. Oh, I'll exchange it.

1.

2.

3.

4.

5.

6.

Color the dress red.   Color the skirt yellow.
Color the pants brown.   Color the socks green.
Color the hat black.   Color the shirt blue.

1.

2.

3.

4.

5.
exchanging
sewing
making

6.
washing
trying on
wearing

179

1. What's _____ doing?

_____ _____ _____ _____ .

2. What's _____ wearing?

_____ _____ _____ _____ .

3. What's _____ doing?

_____ _____ _____ _____ .

4. What's _____ doing?

_____ _____ _____ .

5. What's _____ doing?

_____ _____ _____ _____ .

6. What's _____ doing?

_____ _____ _____ .

A. Can I help you?

B. Yes, I want to exchange this dress.

I want a blue one.

A. Do you have the receipt?

B. Yes, I do.

A.	**Can I help you?**	**What's wrong?**	**Do you have the receipt?**
B.	I want to exchange this _____		
		too small	yes
		too big	no

A. I want to buy this shirt.

B. Cash or charge?

A. Cash.

B. Let's see. $21.00 plus tax.
That's _____ .

A. Here's the money.

B. _____ from $30.00.
Your change is _____ .

CASH OR CHARGE?

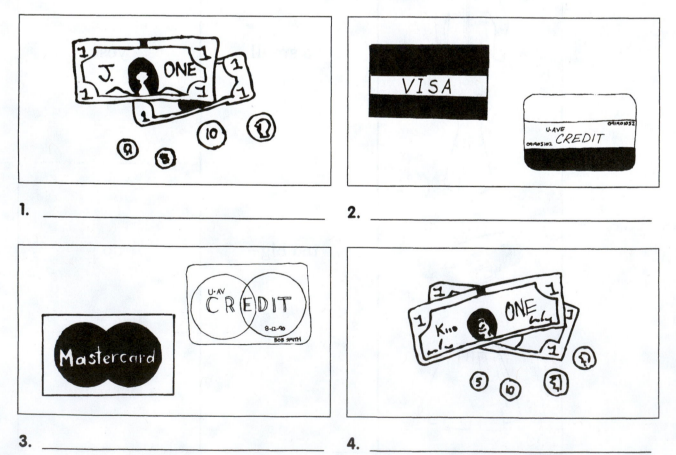

1. _____   2. _____

3. _____   4. _____

| jacket | shirt | socks | hat | shoes |

A.   Can I go outside?

B.   Just a minute.

Pull up your  _____ ,

and tie your _____ .

A.   OK, can I go now?

B.   Just a minute.

Button your 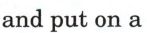 _____ ,

and put on a  _____ .

A.   OK, can I go now?

B.   Just a minute.

Put on a _____
and zip it up.

A.   Can I go now?

B.   Yes, you can.

183

A.   Where are you going?

B.   I'm going to sewing class.

A.   How much is it?

B.   It's free.

A.   What are you making?

B.   I'm making a shirt.

A.   Is it difficult?

B.   No, it isn't. It's easy.

A.   Is it fun?

B.   Yes, it is.

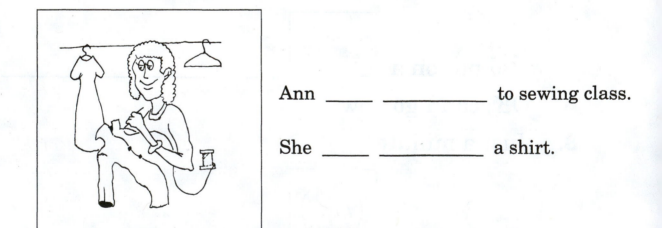

Ann _____ _____ to sewing class.

She _____ _____ a shirt.

1. Pick up the thread.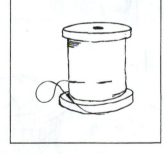

2. Pick up the scissors.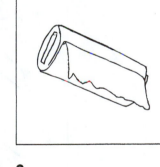

3. Cut the thread.

4. Pick up the needle.

5. Thread the needle.

6. Tie a knot.

7. Put the button on the material.

8. Sew the button on the material.

9. Sew up and down, up and down.

10. Tie a knot.

11. Cut the thread.

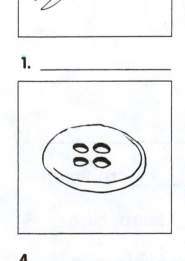

1. _____

2. _____

3. _____

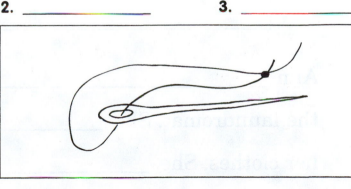

4. _____

5. _____

6. _____

A. Where are you going?

B. I'm going to the laundromat.

I need to wash my clothes.

A. Do you have soap?

B. Yes, I do.

A. Do you have bleach?

B. No, I don't. I don't need bleach.

A. Do you have change for the machines?

B. Yes, I do.

Ann _____ _____ to

the laundromat. She _____ to wash

her clothes. She _____ soap. She

_____ change for the machines.

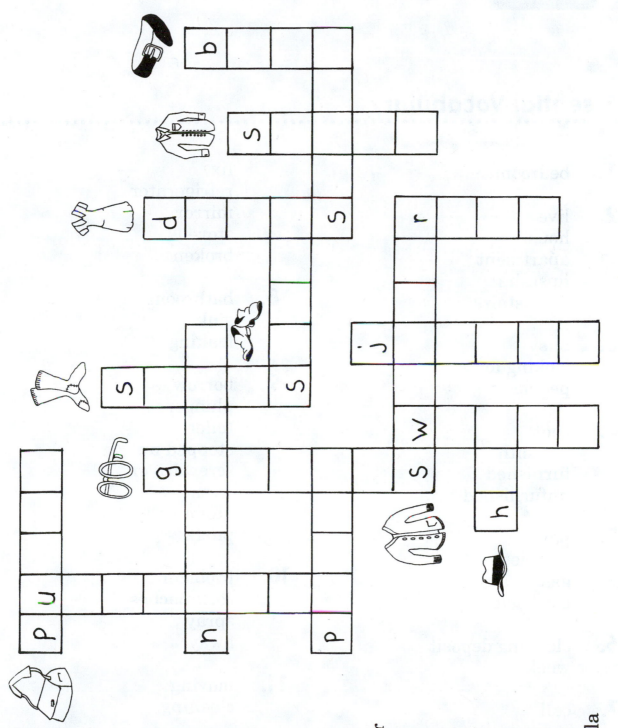

dress
hat
watch
sweater
belt
socks
shoes
purse
pants
jacket
shirt
skirt
glasses
umbrella

8 HOUSING

Essential Vocabulary

1. bedroom

2. live
   house
   apartment
   upstairs
   downstairs

3. busy
   looking for
   people

4. rent
   a month
   furnished
   unfurnished

5. pay
   utilities
   gas
   electricity

6. cleaning deposit
   week

7. call
   manager

fix
refrigerator
mirror
stove
broken

8. bathroom
   sink
   leaking

9. borrow
   plunger
   toilet
   stopped up
   screwdriver
   wrench
   hammer
   pliers

10. problem
    cockroaches
    spray
    away

11. moving
    cleaning

FURNISHED

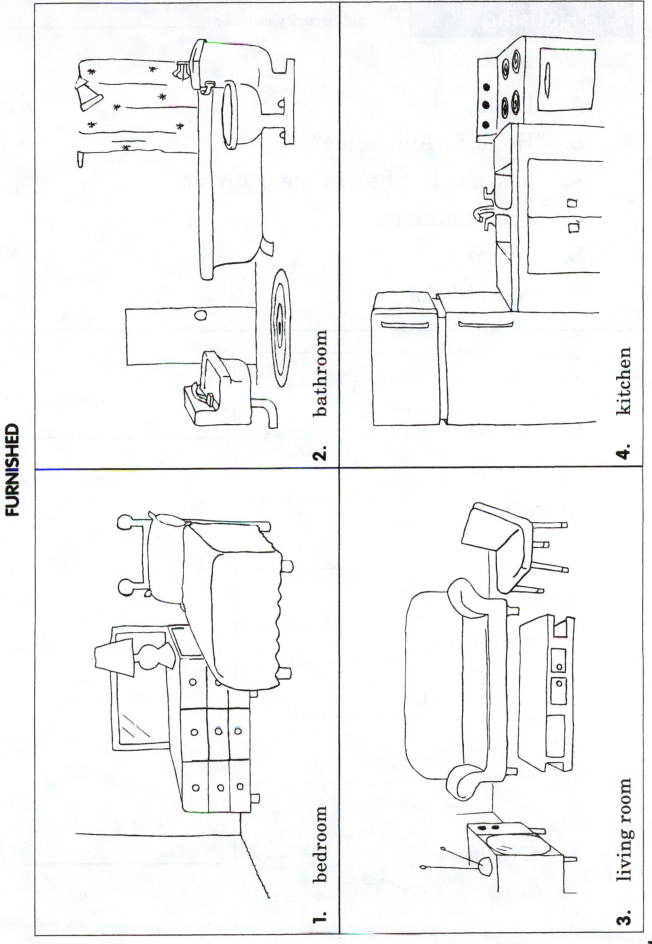

1. bedroom

2. bathroom

3. living room

4. kitchen

A. Hello.

B. Hello. Is Ann home?

A. Yes, she is. She's in the bedroom.
Just a minute.

B. Thanks.

A. Ann, it's for you.

---

1. She's in the  _____.

2. She's in the 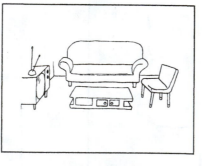 _____.

3. She's in the  _____.

Birth date _____

A. Do you live in a house?

B. No, I don't.

I live in an apartment.

A. Do you live upstairs or downstairs?

B. I live upstairs.

 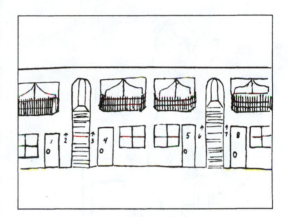

1. Do you live in a house?

_____.

2. Do you live in an apartment?

_____.

3. Do you live upstairs or downstairs?

_____.

4. What's your address?

_____.

5. Do you live with your family?

_____.

1.

2.

3.

4.

5.

6.

fixing
cleaning
thinking

looking
moving
borrowing

A. Hello. How are you?

B. I'm busy. I'm looking for a new apartment.

A. What's the matter?

B. My apartment is too small.

I have 12 people in my family.

I have 1 bedroom.

I need 3 bedrooms.

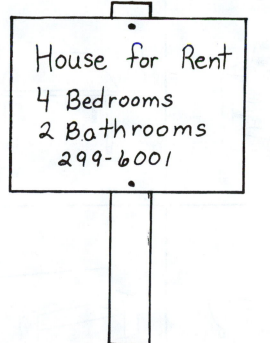

House for Rent
4 Bedrooms
2 Bathrooms
299-6001

1. Is it a house?

_____.

2. How many bedrooms?

_____.

3. How many bathrooms?

_____.

4. What's the telephone number?

_____.

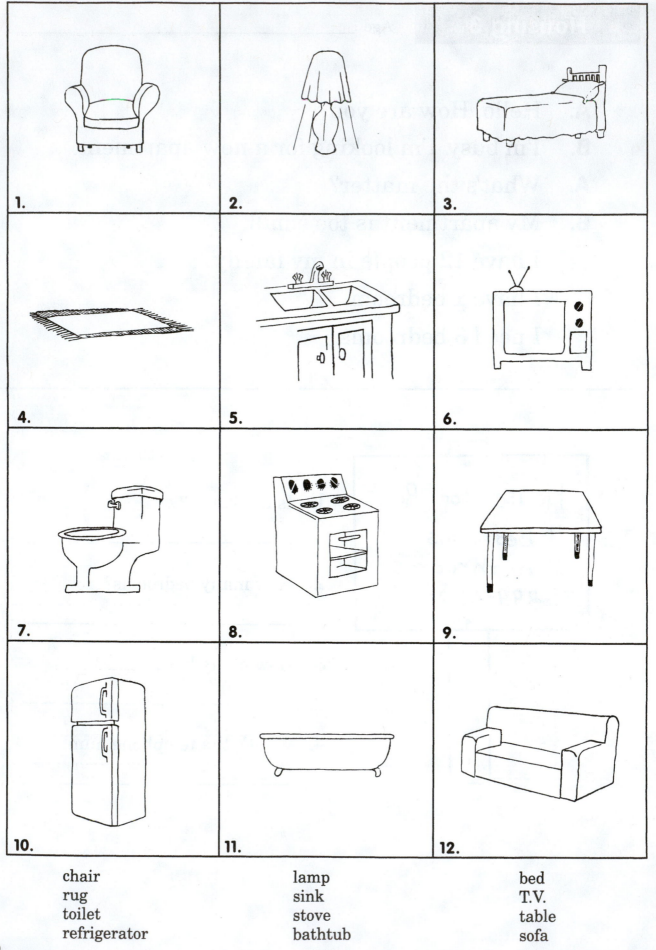

1.

2.

3.

4.

5.

6.

7.

8.

9.

10.

11.

12.

chair   lamp   bed
rug   sink   T.V.
toilet   stove   table
refrigerator   bathtub   sofa

Signature _____

A. I need a 3 bedroom apartment.
Do you have one?

B. Yes, I do.

A. How much is the rent?

B. It's $400 a month.

A. Is it furnished?

B. No, it isn't. It's unfurnished.

A. Thanks.

Match

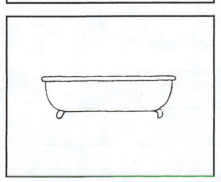

1. sofa

2. stove

3. bathtub

4. refrigerator

5. chair

6. table

Match

apartment	mo.
bedroom	apt.
bathroom	br.
month	ba.

$450 a mo.
1 Br.
1 Ba. apt.

1. How much? _____

2. How many bathrooms? _____

3. How many bedrooms? _____

$395 a mo.
3 Br.
2 Ba.

1. How much? _____

2. How many bedrooms? _____

3. How many bathrooms? _____

For Rent
$850 a mo.
Children OK
4 Br.
2 Ba.

1. How much? _____

2. How many bedrooms? _____

3. How many bathrooms? _____

A. Is this house for rent?

B. Yes, it is. It's $650 a month.

A. How many bedrooms?

B. 3.

A. Do you pay utilities?

B. I pay water.

You pay gas and electricity.

A. Can I see it?

B. Yes, you can.

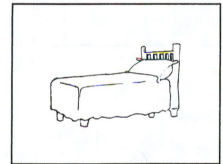

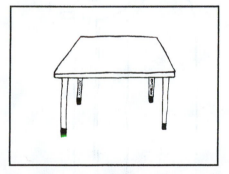

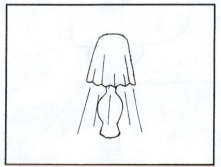

Match

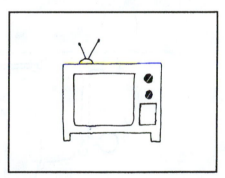

1. lamp

2. bed

3. TV

4. rug

5. toilet

6. table

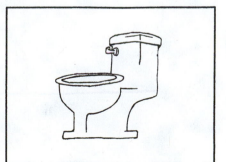

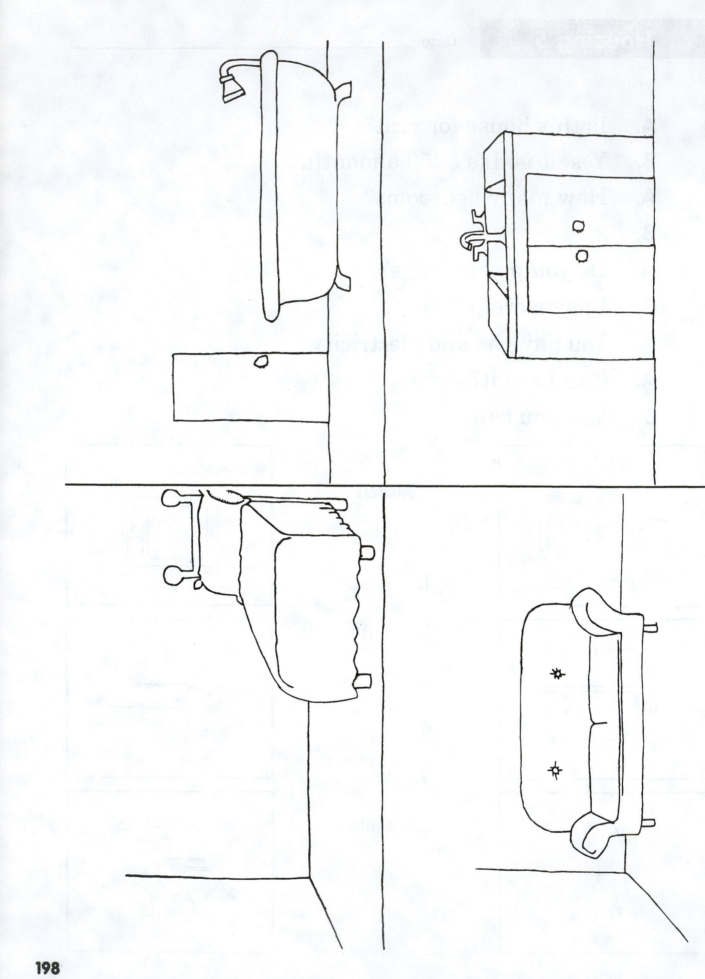

See the Teacher's Guide.

A. How much is the house?

B. It's $460 a month.

A. How much is the cleaning deposit?

B. $200.

A. When can I move in?

B. Next week.

1.	utilities	security deposit
2.	rent	water
3.	gas and lights	house
4.	house	utilities
5.	water	rent
6.	cleaning deposit	gas and lights
7.	apartment	water

See the Teacher's Guide.

First name _____

A. My window is broken.
B. Oh, that's too bad.
    Call the manager.
A. Why?
B. Because he can fix it.

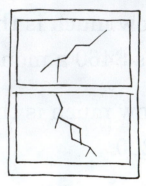

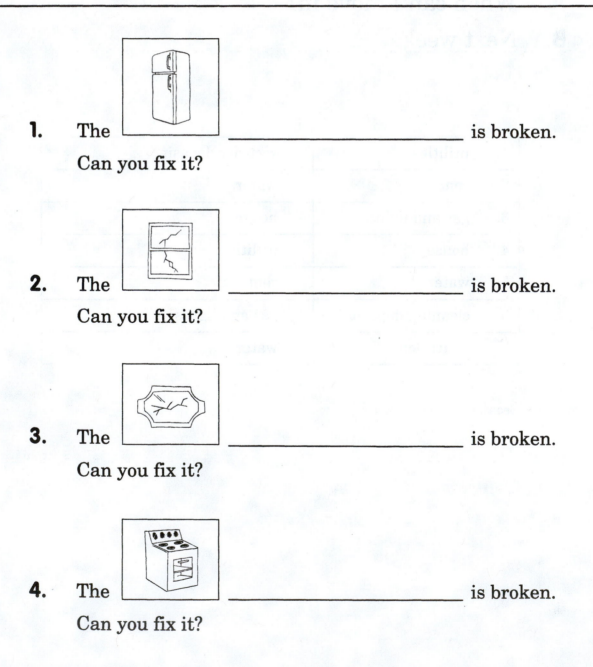

1. The _____ is broken.
    Can you fix it?

2. The _____ is broken.
    Can you fix it?

3. The _____ is broken.
    Can you fix it?

4. The _____ is broken.
    Can you fix it?

A. Hello.

B. Hello. This is _____ .

A. Hi. What's the matter?

B. My bathroom sink is leaking.
Can you fix it?

A. Yes, I can fix it next Tuesday.

B. Thank you. Goodbye.

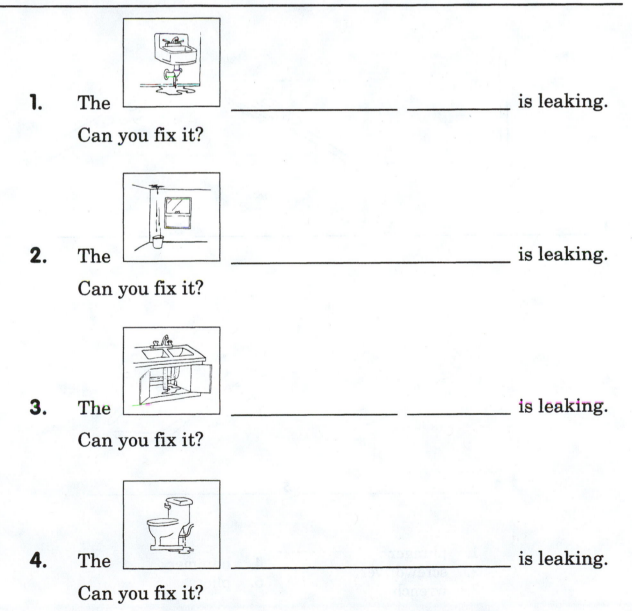

1. The _____ _____ is leaking.
Can you fix it?

2. The _____ is leaking.
Can you fix it?

3. The _____ _____ is leaking.
Can you fix it?

4. The _____ is leaking.
Can you fix it?

A. Hi. Can I borrow your plunger?

B. Sure. What's wrong?

A. My toilet is stopped up.
   I need to fix it.

| Can I borrow your _____ ? |

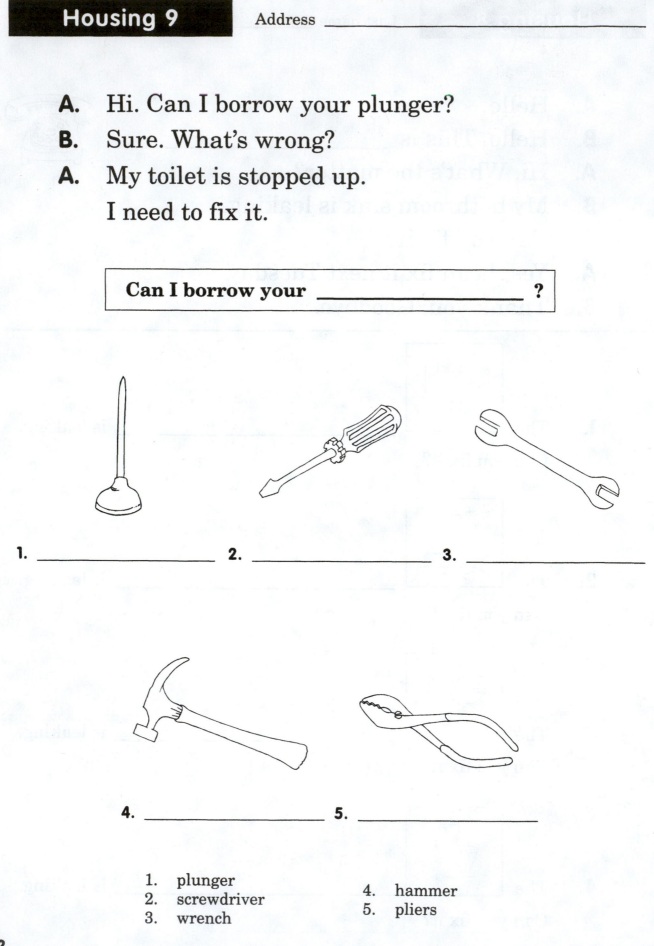

1. _____   2. _____   3. _____

4. _____   5. _____

1. plunger   4. hammer
2. screwdriver   5. pliers
3. wrench

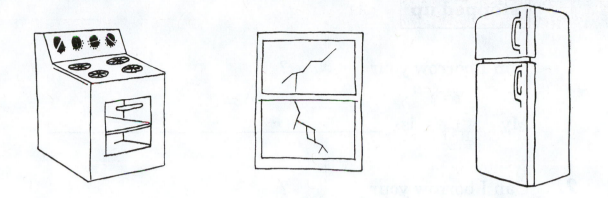

1. The _____ is broken.

2. The _____ is leaking.

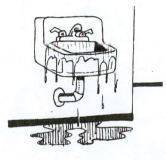
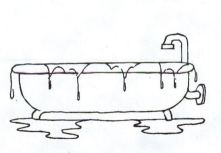

3. The _____ is stopped up.

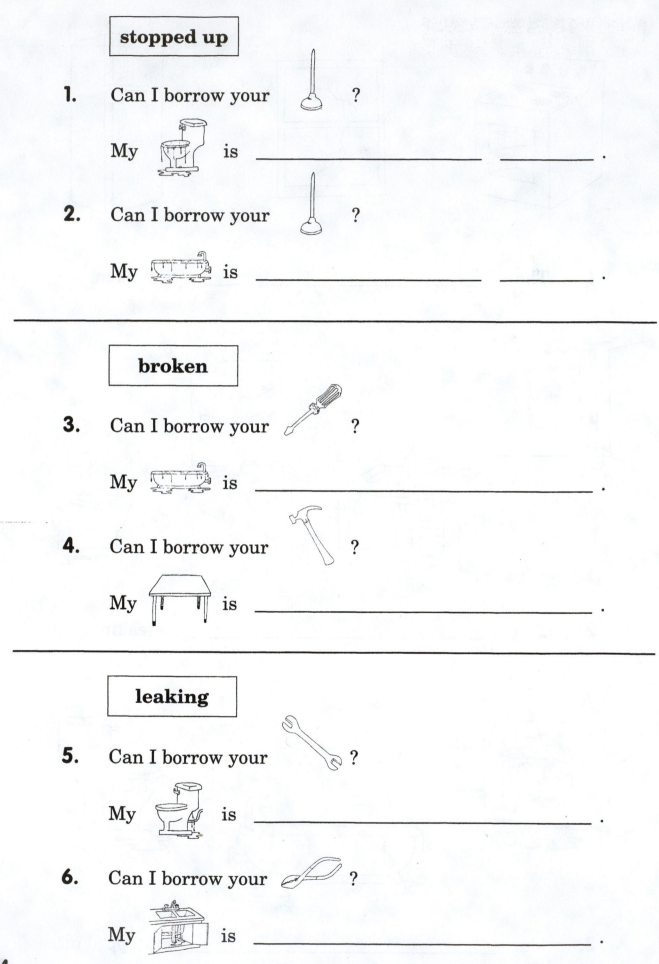

stopped up

1. Can I borrow your   ?

   My   is _____ _____ .

2. Can I borrow your   ?

   My   is _____ _____ .

broken

3. Can I borrow your   ?

   My   is _____ .

4. Can I borrow your   ?

   My   is _____ .

leaking

5. Can I borrow your   ?

   My   is _____ .

6. Can I borrow your   ?

   My   is _____ .

A. Hello.

B. Hello. This is _____ .

I have a problem.

A. What's the matter?

B. I have cockroaches in my apartment.

Can you spray?

A. Yes, I can.

I can spray next Tuesday.

B. Thanks.

A. You need to go away for 4 hours.

B. OK. Goodbye.

A. Bye.

I can spray	tomorrow
	next Wednesday
	next month
	next week
	this Saturday
	this week

Ann has a problem. She has cockroaches in her
kitchen. She has cockroaches in her bathroom, too.
She needs to spray.

1. Who has a problem?

   _____.

2. What's the problem?

   _____.

3. Does Ann have cockroaches?

   _____.

4. Where are the cockroaches?

   _____.

5. Does she need to spray?

   _____.

6. Does she have cockroaches in the living room or the kitchen?

   _____.

Do you have (a) 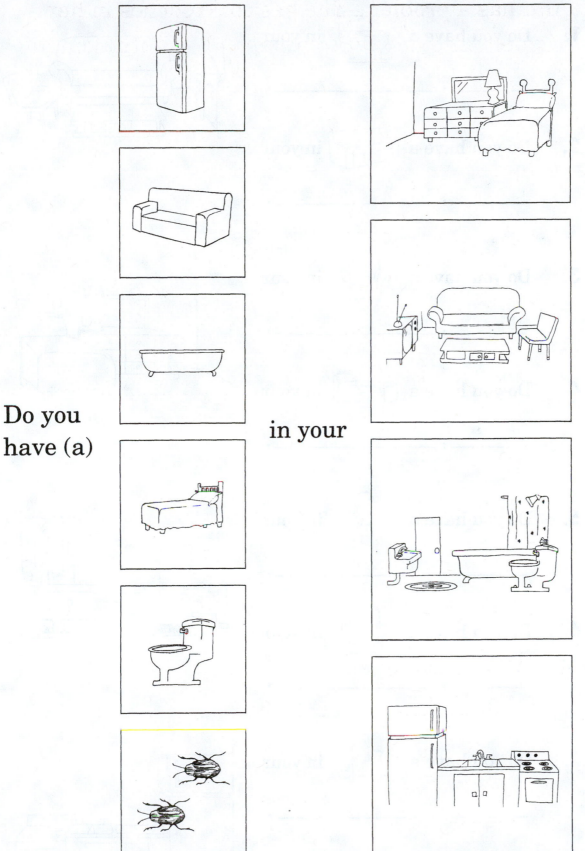 **in your** **?**

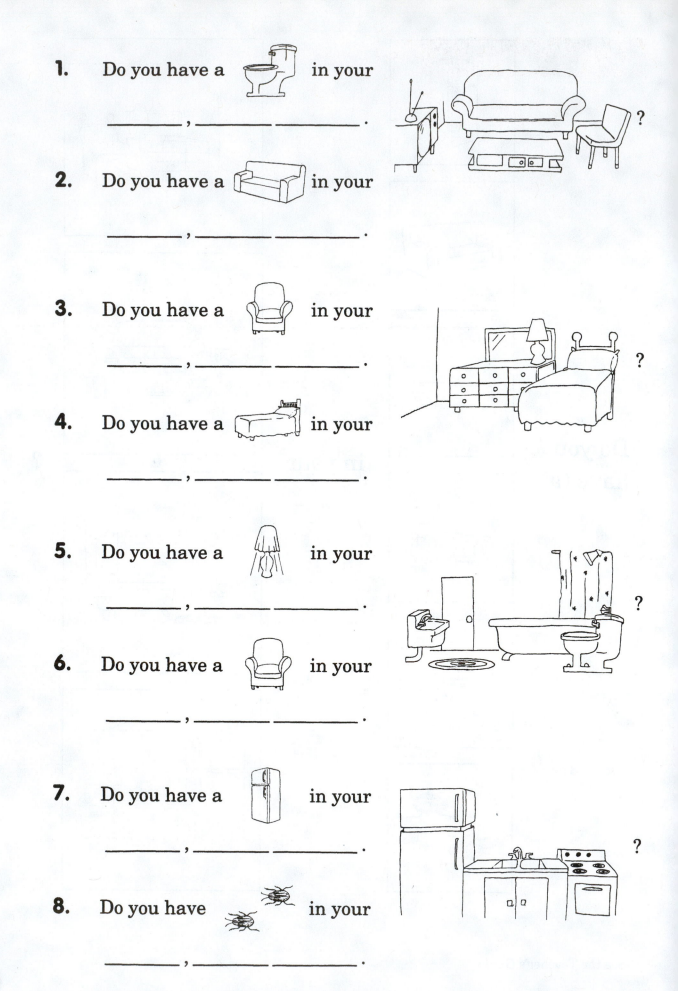

1. Do you have a ⬚ in your

_____ , _____ .

2. Do you have a ⬚ in your

_____ , _____ .

3. Do you have a ⬚ in your

_____ , _____ .

4. Do you have a ⬚ in your

_____ , _____ .

5. Do you have a ⬚ in your

_____ , _____ .

6. Do you have a ⬚ in your

_____ , _____ .

7. Do you have a ⬚ in your

_____ , _____ .

8. Do you have ⬚ in your

_____ , _____ .

A. Are you moving today?

B. No, tomorrow. We're cleaning the apartment today.

A. Why?

B. Because we want our cleaning deposit.

1. I'm cleaning the apartment.

I need a  _____.

2. I'm cleaning the apartment.

I need a  _____.

3. I'm cleaning the apartment.

I need a _____.

4. I'm cleaning the apartment.

I need a _____.

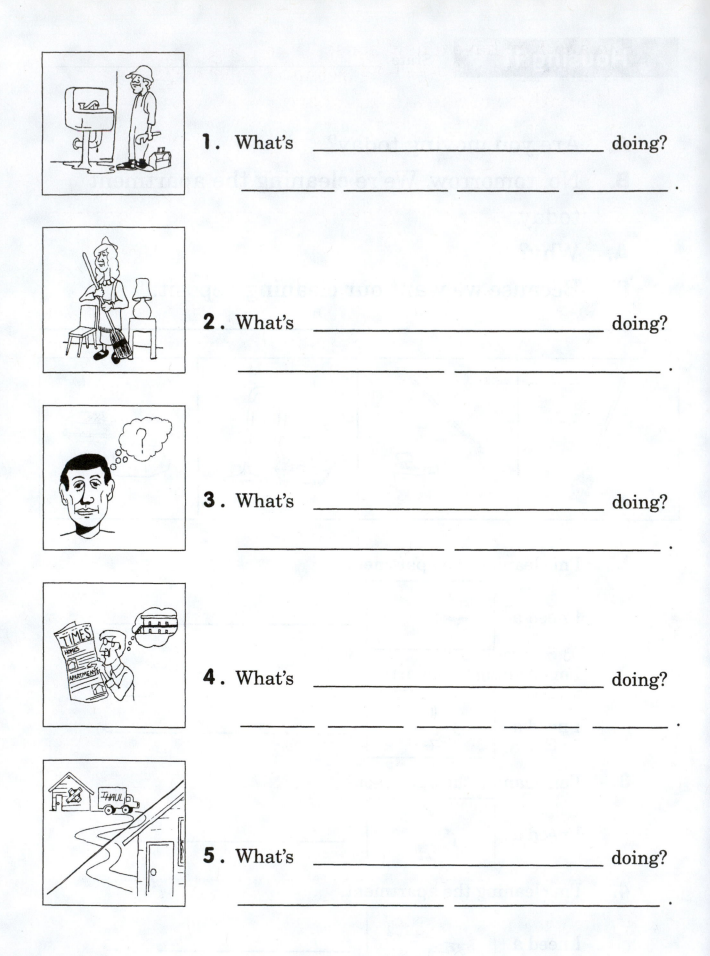

1. What's _____ doing?

_____ .

2. What's _____ doing?

_____ _____ .

3. What's _____ doing?

_____ _____ .

4. What's _____ doing?

_____ _____ _____ _____ _____ .

5. What's _____ doing?

_____ _____ .

Sue and Kim have a new house. It's unfurnished. It has 2 bedrooms and 1 bathroom. Sue and Kim have a sofa, a bed, and a table. They want to buy a refrigerator.

1. Do Sue and Kim have a new house?

   _____.

2. Is it furnished or unfurnished?

   _____.

3. Does it have 2 or 3 bedrooms?

   _____.

4. Do Sue and Kim have a sofa?

   _____.

5. Do Sue and Kim have a bed?

   _____.

6. Do Sue and Kim have a refrigerator?

   _____.

7. Do Sue and Kim want to buy a bed?

   _____.

8. Do Sue and Kim want to buy a table?

   _____.

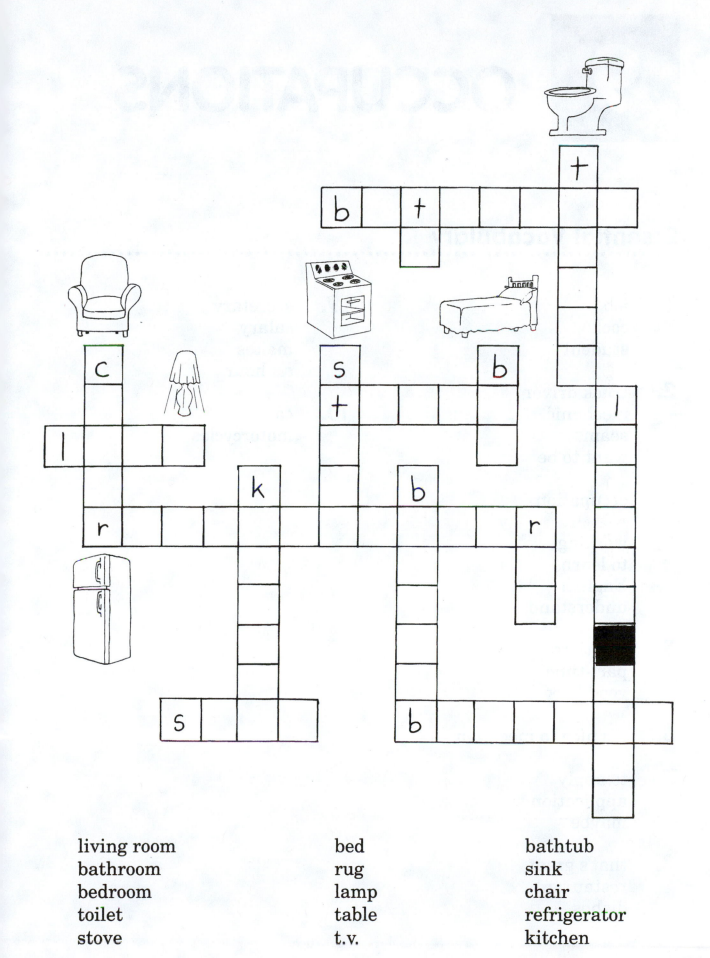

living room   bed   bathtub

bathroom   rug   sink

bedroom   lamp   chair

toilet   table   refrigerator

stove   t.v.   kitchen

OCCUPATIONS

Essential Vocabulary
....

1. job
   cook
   student

2. truck driver
   mechanic
   seamstress
   want to be

3. occupation

4. working
   to learn
   English
   understand

5. full-time
   part-time
   good luck

6. it's nice to meet you

7. to apply
   application
   maybe

8. that's great
   restaurant
   dishes

9. secretary
   salary
   makes
   an hour

10. cars
    motorcycles

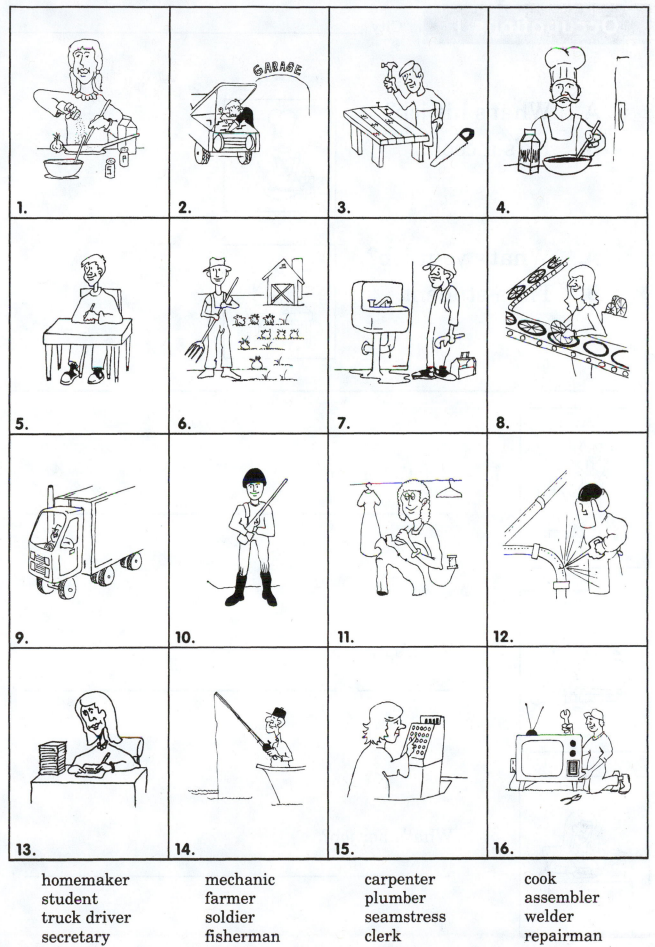

1.

2.

GARAGE

3.

4.

5.

6.

7.

8.

9.

10.

11.

12.

13.

14.

15.

16.

homemaker	mechanic	carpenter	cook
student	farmer	plumber	assembler
truck driver	soldier	seamstress	welder
secretary	fisherman	clerk	repairman

215

A. What's his job?
B. He's a cook.

A. What's your job?
B. I'm a student.

1. What's her job?

_____ _____ _____.

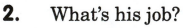

2. What's his job?

_____ _____ _____.

3. What's her job?

_____ _____ _____.

A.   Is he a truck driver?

B.   No, he isn't. He's a mechanic.

A.   Is she a cook?

B.   No, she isn't. She's a seamstress.

A.   Are you a student?

B.   Yes, I am. I want to be a _____.

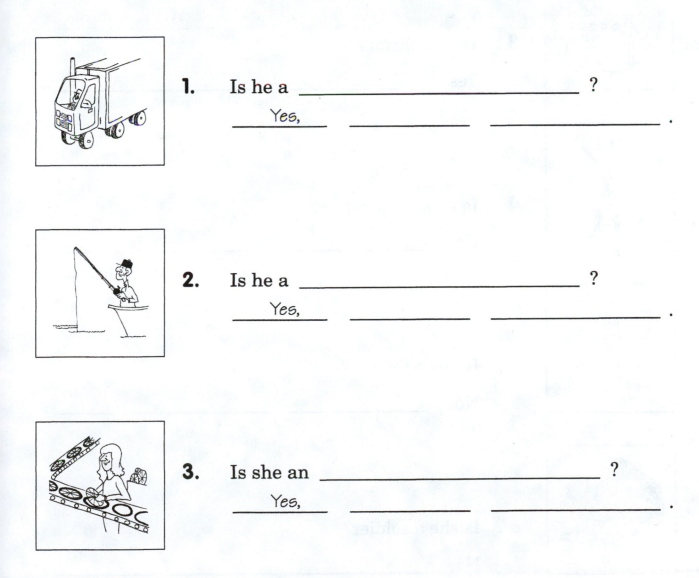

1.   Is he a _____ ?

   _____ Yes, _____ _____ .

2.   Is he a _____ ?

   _____ Yes, _____ _____ .

3.   Is she an _____ ?

   _____ Yes, _____ _____ .

1. Is she a homemaker?

Yes, _____ _____.

2. Is he a mechanic?

Yes, _____ _____.

3. Is he a farmer?

Yes, _____ _____.

4. Is he an assembler?

No, _____ _____.

5. Is she a farmer?

No, _____ _____.

6. Is she a soldier?

No, _____ _____.

A. Where are you from?

B. I'm from _____ .

A. What was your occupation?

B. What?

A. What was your job?

B. I was a _____ .

_____

1. What was his occupation?

_____ _____ _____ _____ .

2. What was her occupation?

_____ _____ _____ _____ .

3. What was his occupation?

_____ _____ _____ _____ .

A. Are you working?

B. No, I'm not.

A. Why?

B. Because I want to learn English.

A. Oh, I understand.

1. Is he working?

   No, _____ _____ .

   Why?

   He wants to _____ _____ .

2. Is he working?

   Yes, _____ _____ .

   What's his job?

   _____ _____ _____ .

3. Is she working?

   Yes, _____ _____ .

   What's her job?

   _____ _____ _____ .

Kim is a student now. He was a soldier in Vietnam. Kim goes to school every day. He studies English. He wants to be a welder.

1. Who's a student?

   _____.

2. Who was a soldier?

   _____.

3. Where is Kim from?

   _____.

4. What was his job?

   _____.

5. What's his job now?

   _____.

6. Is he a welder?

   _____.

7. Is he a fisherman?

   _____.

8. Is he a mechanic?

   _____.

9. Is he a cook?

   _____.

10. Is he a student?

   _____.

A. Are you working?

B. No, I'm not. I'm looking for a job.

A. Full-time or part-time?

B. Part-time.

A. Good luck.

B. Thanks.

He isn't working.

He's looking for a job.

He wants to work full-time.

1. Is he working?

_____.

2. Is he looking for a job?

_____.

3. Does he want full-time or part-time?

_____.

Who	Was	Is

1.

2.

3.

See the Teacher's Guide.

A. This is my friend, _____ .
He's looking for a job.
B. It's nice to meet you, _____ .
C. It's nice to meet you, too.

Ann

A. This is my friend, _____ .
B. It's _____ _____ _____ _____ ,

_____ .

Bob

A. This is my friend, _____ .
B. It's _____ _____ _____ _____ ,

_____ .

Kim

A. This is my friend, _____ .
B. It's _____ _____ _____ _____ ,

_____ .

Lee

A. This is my friend, _____ .
B. It's _____ _____ _____ _____ ,

_____ .

Bob Jones wants to apply for a job. He has the application. His address is 3617 Main Street, San Diego, California. His zip code is 92110. He's 35 years old. His birth date is May 17, 1958. His telephone number is 555–7639.

JOB APPLICATION

Last name _____ First name _____

Address _____ City _____

State _____ Zip code _____

Telephone _____ Soc. Sec. No. _____

Bob Jones is from Mexico. His Social Security number is 560–58–8025. He's married. He has 4 children. He was a mechanic in Mexico for ten years. He wants full-time work.

SEX: male ☐	female ☐	
Are you over 18 years old? yes ☐		no ☐
Do you want full-time? ☐ part-time? ☐		
What was your job? _____		
How long at this job? _____		
Signature _____		
Date _____		

A. I want to apply for a job.

B. Here's the application.

Please fill it out.

A. Can I return it tomorrow?

B. Yes, you can.

A. Can I help you?

B. Yes, I want to return my job application.

A. Thank you.

B. Can I come for an interview?

A. Maybe. We'll call you.

B. OK. Thank you.

JOB APPLICATION

Last name _____   First name _____

Address _____   City _____

State _____   Zip code _____

How long at this address?_____

Telephone _____   Soc. Sec. No. _____

SEX: male ☐   female ☐

Are you over 18 years old?   yes ☐   no ☐

Do you want full-time? ☐   part-time? ☐

What was your job? _____

How long at this job?_____

Signature _____

Date _____

---

1.   Fill out this application in ink.

2.   Please print.

3.   Remember to sign your name.

A. I have a new job.

B. That's great.

What do you do?

A. I work in a restaurant.

B. Do you wash dishes?

A. No, I don't. I cook.

A. She has a new job.

B. What does she do?

A. She sews.

A. He has a new job.

B. What does he do?

A. He fixes cars.

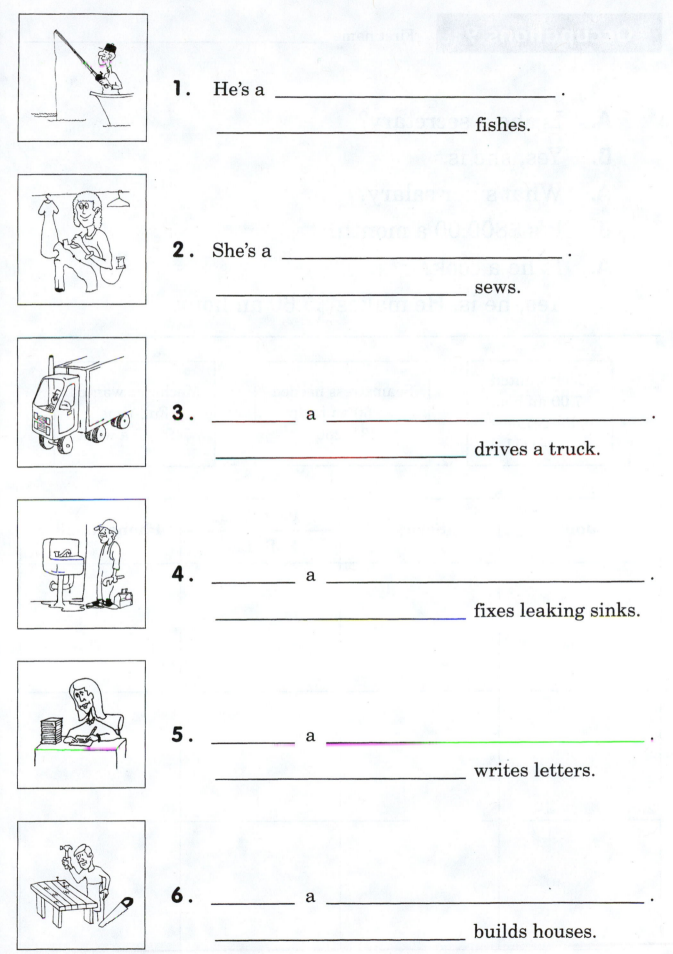

1. He's a _____.

_____ fishes.

2. She's a _____.

_____ sews.

3. _____ a _____ _____.

_____ drives a truck.

4. _____ a _____.

_____ fixes leaking sinks.

5. _____ a _____.

_____ writes letters.

6. _____ a _____.

_____ builds houses.

First name _____

A. Is she a secretary?

B. Yes, she is.

A. What's her salary?

B. It's $800.00 a month.

A. Is he a cook?

B. Yes, he is. He makes $5.60 an hour.

1.
Cook wanted
$7.00 an hour
Part-time
292–1111

2.
Seamstress needed
$5.50 an hour
731–2864

3.
Mechanic wanted
Full-time
$490.00 a week

Job	Salary	Part-time / Full-time	Phone number
1.			
2.			
3.			

Last name _____

A. My son wants a job.

B. What can he do?

A. He can fix cars.

B. Can he fix motorcycles, too?

A. Yes, he can. He's a mechanic.

---

1. She's a _____ .

_____ can write letters.

2. She's a _____ .

_____ can cook.

3. He's a _____ .

_____ can farm.

Juan was a mechanic in Mexico. He's
a student now. He's looking for a job.
He can fix cars. He can work part-time.

1. Who was a mechanic?

   _____.

2. Who's a student now?

   _____.

3. Was Juan a mechanic in Mexico?

   _____.

4. Is Juan a student now?

   _____.

5. Is Juan looking for a job?

   _____.

6. What can he do?

   _____.

7. Can he fix cars?

   _____.

8. Can he work part-time?

   _____.

9. Can he work full-time?

   _____.

10. What was his job?

   _____.

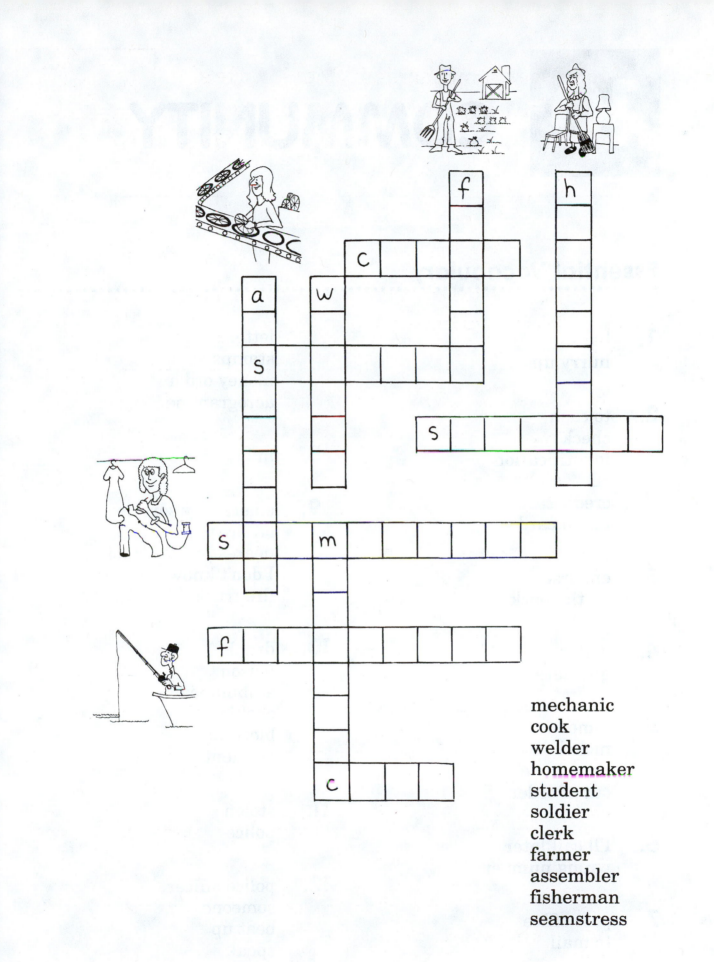

mechanic
cook
welder
homemaker
student
soldier
clerk
farmer
assembler
fisherman
seamstress

233

10 COMMUNITY

Essential Vocabulary

1. bank
   hurry up

2. to cash
   check
   identification
   ID
   credit card
   green card

3. endorse
   on the back

4. dollar
   quarters

5. dimes
   nickel
   pay phone
   out of order

6. I'll call later
   wrong number

7. post office
   to mail

letter
stamps
money order
aerogramme

8. in line

9. emergency services
   on fire
   nearest cross street
   I don't know
   fire truck

10. drank
    poison
    ambulance
    choking
    bleeding
    accident

11. stolen
    police

12. police officer
    someone
    beat up
    speak

13. bill
advertisement
throw it away

14. gas and electric
service charge
total

15. library card
sign

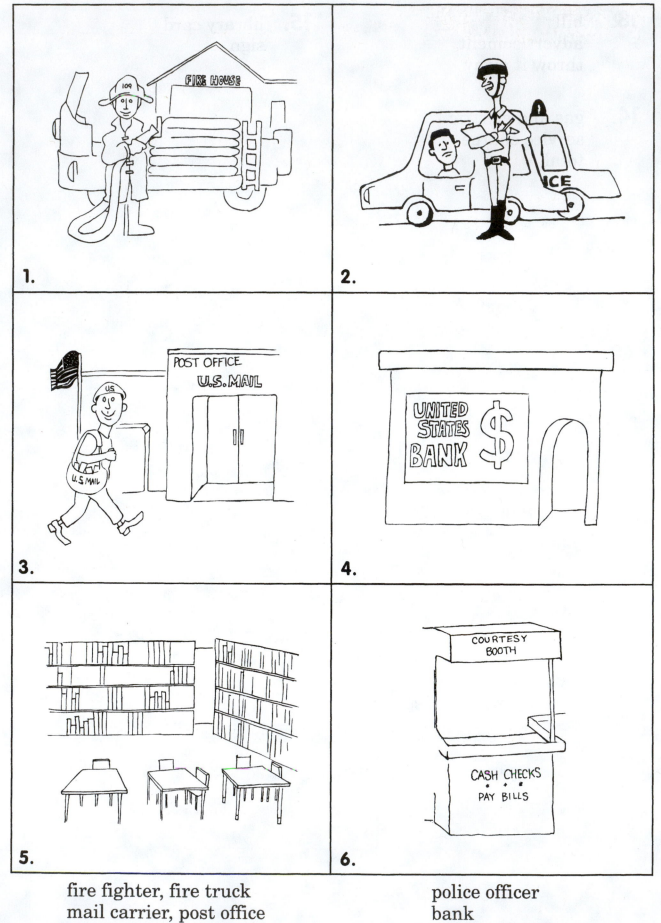

fire fighter, fire truck
mail carrier, post office
library

police officer
bank
courtesy booth

A. Hello.

B. Hi.

A. Where are you going?

B. I'm going to the bank.

A. Is it open?

B. Yes, it opens at 10:00 and closes at 5:00.

A. Oh, hurry up. It's 4:30 now.

	open	*closed*
Mon.	10:00	5:00
Tue.	10:00	5:00
Wed.	10:00	5:00
Thur.	10:00	5:00
Fri.	10:00	8:00
Sat.	9:00	12:00
Sun.	CLOSED	

1. What time does the bank open on Tuesday?

_____ .

2. What time does the bank open on Saturday?

_____ .

3. What time does the bank close on Friday?

_____ .

Store Hours	
Sun.	closed
Mon.	10–5
Tues.	10–5
Wed.	10–5
Thurs.	9–5
Fri.	9–7
Sat	9–1

1. Is the store open on Monday?

   _____ , _____ _____ .

2. What time is it open on Monday?

   _____ .

3. Is the store open on Friday?

   _____ , _____ _____ .

4. What time is it open on Friday?

   _____ .

5. Is the store open on Sunday?

   _____ , _____ _____ .

6. When is it open on Saturday?

   _____–_____ .

7. When is it open on Tuesday?

   _____–_____ .

8. When is it open on Wednesday?

   _____–_____ .

A. Next.

B. I want to cash my check.

A. Do you have identification?

B. What?

A. Do you have ID?

B. Oh. Yes, I do.

1. _____   2. _____

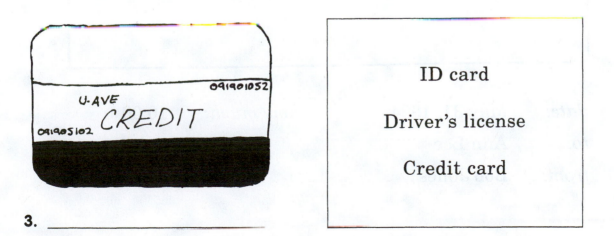

3. _____

ID card

Driver's license

Credit card

A. I want to cash this check.
Here's my ID.

B. It's $3.00 to cash a check.

A. $3.00?

B. Yes, $3.00.

A. Oh, OK.

B. Please endorse the check.

A. What?

B. Write your name on the back.

```
┌─────────────────────────────────────────────────────┐
│                                                       │
│                              _____ 19_____      │
│   Pay to the                            ┌──────────┐  │
│   order of                            $ │          │  │
│   _____ └──────────┘  │
│                                                       │
│   _____ Dollars    │
│                                                       │
│                           _____      │
│                                                       │
└─────────────────────────────────────────────────────┘
```

date: May 31, 1994   *how much:*   10.00

to: Ann Lee   ten

from: Bob Jones

Pay to the order of **Gas and Electric**   June 18 19 84 $ 54.98

Fifty-four and 98/100 —————————— Dollars

Ann Lee

1. Who's it to? _____

2. Who's it from? _____

3. How much? _____

4. What's the date? _____

Pay to the order of **Telephone Company**   Dec. 3 19 83 $ 13.67

Thirteen and 67/100 —————————— Dollars

Bob Jones

5. Who's it to? _____

6. Who's it from? _____

7. How much? _____

8. What's the date? _____

1.

_____ 19 _____

Pay to the
order of _____ $ [   ]

_____ Dollars

_____

2.

_____ 19 _____

Pay to the
order of _____ $ [   ]

_____ Dollars

_____

3.

_____ 19 _____

Pay to the
order of _____ $ [   ]

_____ Dollars

_____

Mr. Jones is in the bank. He has a check.
He wants to cash the check. He wants
money. He's endorsing the check on the
back.

1. Where's Mr. Jones?

   _____.

2. Does he have a check?

   _____.

3. Does he want to cash a check?

   _____.

4. Does he want money?

   _____.

5. Where does he endorse the check?

   _____.

6. Who's in the bank?

   _____.

7. What does he have?

   _____.

8. Please sign your name.

   _____.

9. Please write your name.

   _____.

A. Excuse me. Do you have change for a dollar?

B. What do you need?

A. I need 4 quarters.

B. Let me see. Sorry, I don't.

A. Thanks, anyway.

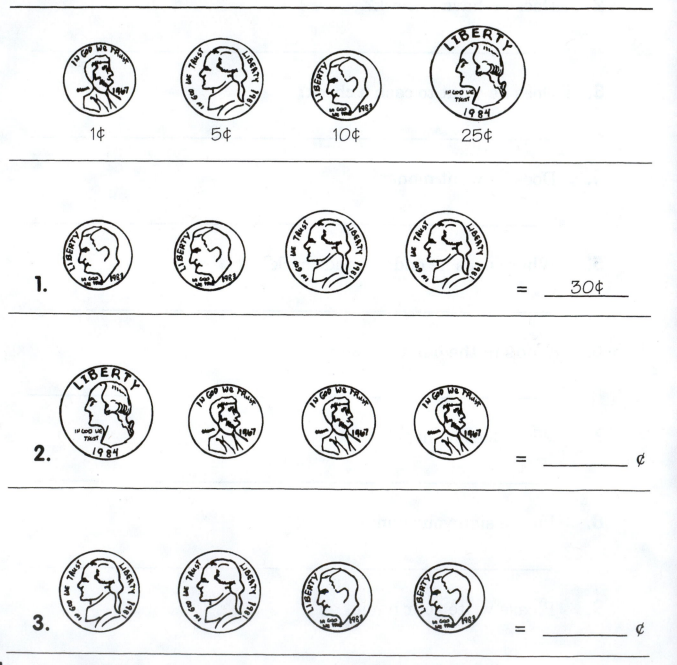

1¢   5¢   10¢   25¢

1. = ___30¢___

2. = _____ ¢

3. = _____ ¢

A. Do you have change for a quarter?

B. Yes, I do. I have 2 dimes and a nickel.

A. Thanks. Do you have a pay phone?

B. Yes, but it's out of order.

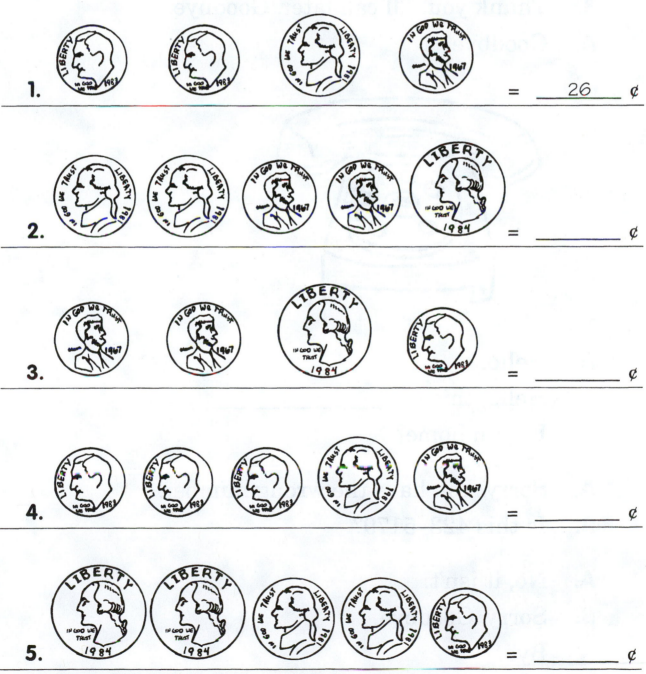

1. _____ = ___26___ ¢

2. _____ = _____ ¢

3. _____ = _____ ¢

4. _____ = _____ ¢

5. _____ = _____ ¢

A. Hello.

B. Hello, this is _____ .
Is Bob home?

A. No, he isn't. He's at school.

B. Thank you. I'll call later. Goodbye.

A. Goodbye.

A. Hello.

B. Hello, this is _____ .
Is Ann home?

A. Sorry. You have the wrong number.

B. Is this 423–5179?

A. No, it isn't.

B. Sorry. Goodbye.

A. Bye.

A. I'm going to the post office.

I need to mail a letter.

B. Can I come? I need to buy stamps.

A. OK. Let's go.

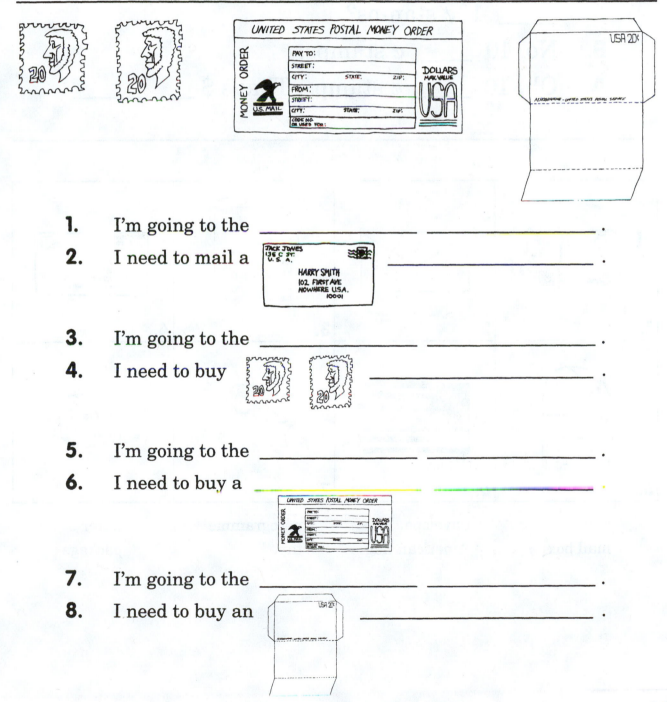

1. I'm going to the _____ _____ .

2. I need to mail a _____ .

3. I'm going to the _____ _____ .

4. I need to buy _____ .

5. I'm going to the _____ _____ .

6. I need to buy a _____ .

7. I'm going to the _____ _____ .

8. I need to buy an _____ .

A.   Are you in line?

B.   Yes.

A.   You're next.

B.   I want to buy 10 _____ ¢ stamps.

A.   _____ 10¢ stamps?

B.   No, 10 _____ ¢ stamps.

A.   Oh, 10 _____ ¢ stamps. That's $ _____ .

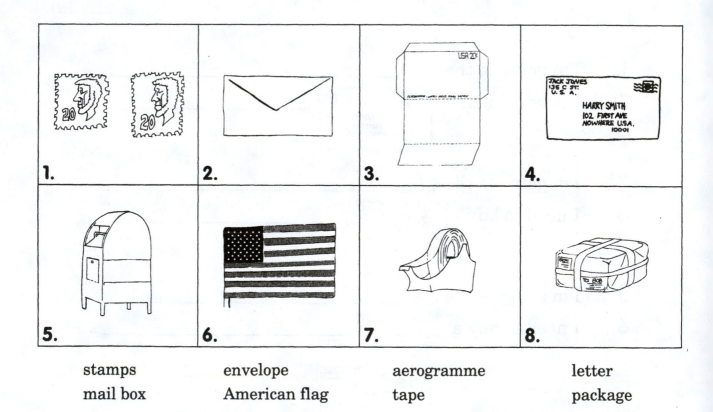

stamps	envelope	aerogramme	letter
mail box	American flag	tape	package

```
Tom  Smith
4373 East Street
Chicago, IL 59210                                    [stamp]

                    Bob  Jones
        Air Mail    7613 Main Street
                    San Diego CA 92111
```

1. Who's it to? _____

2. Who's it from? _____

3. What's Tom's address? _____

_____

4. What's Bob's address? _____

_____

```
Sue White
9379 "A" Long Ave.
Los Angeles CA 92178                                 [stamp 20¢]

                Ann Lee
                6514  First Street
                New York, N.Y 74920
```

5. Who's it to? _____

6. Who's it from? _____

7. What's Ann's zip code? _____

8. How much is the stamp? _____

911

A. Emergency Services.

B. I need help.

My kitchen is on fire.

A. What's your address?

B. _____ .

A. What's your nearest cross street?

B. I don't know.

A. OK. A fire truck is coming.

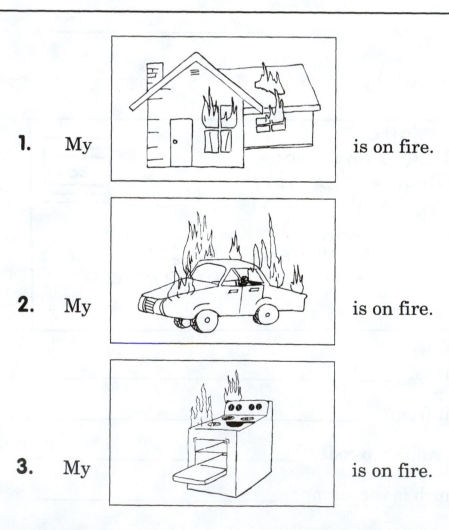

1. My _____ is on fire.

2. My _____ is on fire.

3. My _____ is on fire.

911

A.   Emergency Services.

B.   This is an emergency.
        My son drank poison.

A.   What's your name?

B.   _____ .

A.   What's your address?

B.   _____ .

A.   What's your nearest cross street?

B.   _____ .

A.   OK. An ambulance is coming.

B.   Thank you.

1.   choking   **2.**   accident   **3.**   poison   **4.**   bleeding

A. My purse was stolen.

B. Oh no! Call the police.

A. What's the number?

B. _____

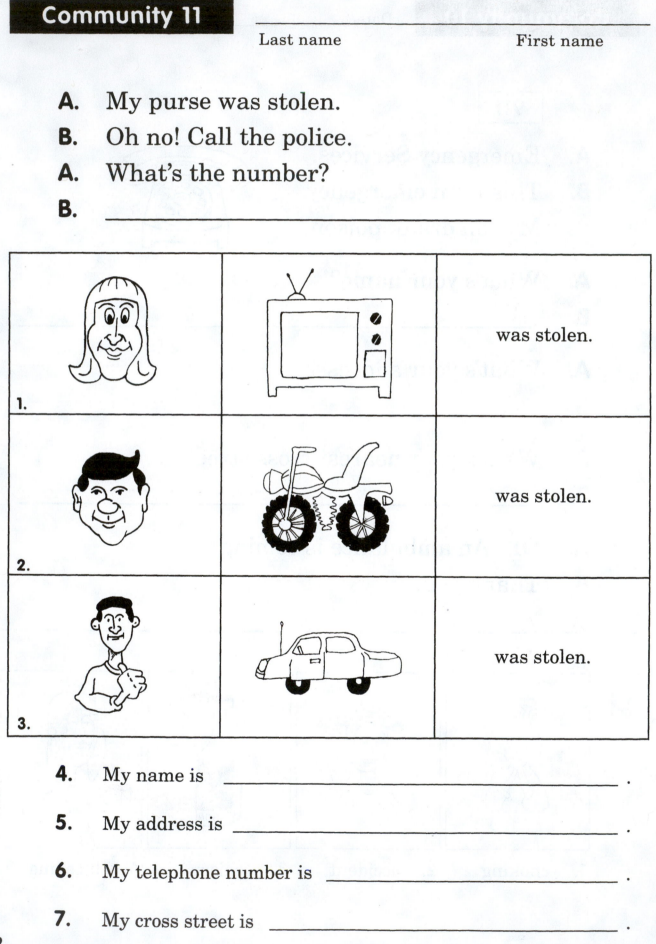

1.   was stolen.

2.   was stolen.

3.   was stolen.

4. My name is _____ .

5. My address is _____ .

6. My telephone number is _____ .

7. My cross street is _____ .

911

A. Emergency Services.

B. Hello. I need a police officer.
This is an emergency.

A. What's the matter?

B. Someone beat up my son.

I'm from _____.

I speak _____.

A. What's your name?

B. _____.

A. What's your address?

B. _____.

A. A police officer is coming.

B. Thank you.

City   State

A. Here's the mail.

B. This is a bill. I need to pay it.

A. Is this a bill?

B. No, it isn't. It's an advertisement.
Throw it away.

Bayside Telephone Company	From *3/28* to *4/28*

Bob Jones   Account Number 8377–664–921
3613 Main St.
San Diego, CA

Monthly Service Charge $10.88
U.S. Tax   .64
Total $11.52

Payment for current charges is due *June 13*.

---

1. Who's it to? _____ .

2. Who's it from? _____ .

3. How much is the bill? _____ .

4. When is it due? _____ .

Nadia and her family are new in the United States. It is difficult for them to understand their bills. Every month the bills come. Every month they pay the bills. They pay for food, rent, utilities, and clothing.

---

1. Is it difficult for Nadia and her family to understand their bills?

    _____.

2. Are Nadia and her family new to the United States?

    _____.

3. Do the bills come every week?

    _____.

4. Do the bills come every month?

    _____.

5. Do they pay their bills every month?

    _____.

6. Do your bills come every month?

    _____.

7. Do you pay your rent every month?

    _____.

8. Do you pay your utilities every month?

    _____.

9. Is it difficult for you to understand your bills?

    _____.

State   Zip code

A. Can I pay my gas and electric bill here?

B. Yes, you can.

A. How much is the service charge?

B. 50¢. Let me see your bill.

   It's $44.00. The total is $44.50.

191567823001	7613 Main St.	Total $39.28

Pirate Gas and Electric Co.
Service from *7/28* to *8/28*

Gas	26	Therms	12.56
Elec.	258	KWHR	26.05
Gas Franchise Fee			.13
Elec. Franchise Fee			.54

	Due Sept. 22, 1993	Total $39.28

1. How much is the bill? _____ .

2. When is it due?_____ .

3. Who is it from? _____ .

Birth date   Age

A. Can I help you?

B. Yes, I want this book.

A. Do you have a library card?

B. No, I don't.

A. Do you have ID?

B. Yes, I do.

A. OK. I can give you a card. Here it is. Sign your name.

LIBRARY CARD

Name _____

Address _____

_____

Signature_____

Telephone _____ Driver's lic. no. _____

Parent's signature _____

---

1. Do you have a library card?

_____.

2. Do you go to the library?

_____.

Kim likes the library. He likes to read. He has a library card. He can take books home. Some books are difficult. Some books are easy. He can read the easy books now.

1. Does Kim like the library?

   _____.

2. Does Kim like to read?

   _____.

3. Does Kim have a library card?

   _____.

4. Can Kim take books home?

   _____.

5. Can Kim read easy books?

   _____.

6. Can you read easy books?

   _____.

7. Do you like to read?

   _____.

8. Do you like the library?

   _____.

9. Do you have a library card?

   _____.

1. OPEN | CLOSED

2. IN | OUT

3. ENTRANCE | EXIT

4. PULL | PUSH

5. OUT OF ORDER

6. TRASH

7. FIRE ALARM EMERGENCY PULL

8. (no smoking)

9. MEN | RESTROOMS | WOMEN

open / close
push / pull
fire alarm

in / out
out of order
no smoking

entrance / exit
trash
men / women